CAN YOU MANAGE?

Everything you need to know
about managing club teams
in Gaelic football, hurling
and other sports

Tim Healy

Ballpoint Press

**Liverpool joke
Spring 2010**

*Rafa Benitez sees an old lady about to cross the
street, laden down with bags of groceries.*

Rafa: "Can you manage?"

*Old lady: "Sod off mate. You created the mess.
Get yourself out of it."*

ABOUT THE AUTHOR

Tim Healy has had a lifelong involvement with the GAA as player, coach, manager and administrator. Born in Cork, he captained Coláiste Chríost Rí to their first ever Munster colleges senior football title. He played minor football for Cork and senior football for Wicklow. He has coached and managed successful Bray Emmets teams as well as managing the senior footballers of Castletown of Wexford and UCD. Tim has also managed the Wicklow under-21 football team.

A former executive director of Glen Abbey plc and managing director of his own business for over a quarter of a century, the author brings his Masters of Business Administration (MBA) experience and understanding of business management into the sporting arena with clearly defined methods and techniques designed as a blueprint for aspiring managers of club teams.

For Clare
and for Barbara, Clare C and Patrick

A LETTER FROM THE GAA PRESIDENT

Cumann Lúthchleas Gael provides fertile ground for academics and authors seeking to explore and understand the workings and nuances of this great sporting and cultural organisation.

The evolution of the modern-day inter-county team manager has been well documented through various intriguing biographies and autobiographies, however, we know little of those charged with leading their team down the long and winding roads offered by club level competition.

In this regard, this new book by Tim Healy is a welcome addition to the growing library of GAA-related publications.

The tradition of clubs and their competitions lie at the core of what makes the association the national and international success it continues to be. Taking up the challenge to manage a team at club level ensures that tradition will continue into the future.

This book will make interesting reading for anyone involved in that challenge.

Criostóir Ó Cuana
Uachtarán Chumann Lúthchleas Gael

Published in 2011 by Ballpoint Press
4 Wyndham Park, Bray, Co Wicklow, Republic of Ireland.
Telephone: 086 8217631
Email: ballpointpress1@gmail.com

ISBN 978-0-9550298-4-4

Book design and production by Elly Design

Printed and bound by GraphyCems

CONTENTS

FOREWORD
By Eugene McGee

The GAA could cover every inter-county pitch in the country with coaching certificates awarded over the past 40-odd years since the first official coaching course was held in Gormanston College in 1964 organised by among others Joe Lennon, Frankie Byrne, Jim McKeever and the late Eamon Young.

Thousands have been presented with these certificates following various courses at different levels during that time so we could be excused for thinking that Gaelic games must be the best coached sport in Ireland. Unfortunately that is far from the reality. Of all the thousands of coaching certificate holders in every county, the vast majority have never even coached their own underage club teams.

The underlying reason for this is that coaching a team sport in itself is not sufficient to achieve the desired aims that inspired the GAA in those far-off days to bravely initiate modern coaching methods of the time. The vital other critical element on which coaching depends is the ability of the coach to also *manage* the overall operation of achieving success with the team.

It is only when all the non-coaching aspects of preparing a football or hurling team i.e. MANAGEMENT, are handled properly that the end product of coaching can be successful.

It is the failure to understand good management and put it into practice as part of the coaching package that explains why this country is littered with redundant coaching certificates and frustrated attendees at coaching courses. One has only to look at the method of appointing inter county and club managers to see the futility of what goes on. Invariably when a county or club committee goes looking for a manager the first choice will be to seek out former famous players who might 'look' to have the makings of a team manager.

The GAA is littered with the bodies of failed managers whose reputations as players withered on the rocks of failed management ability.

Therefore when Tim Healy meditated on and observed these developments over many years and at all levels from top to bottom in the GAA, he went about setting some parameters for establishing the role of the manager as a vital component of the whole team preparation package.

This book is a first in the GAA because it quantifies the qualities required to be a manager in the real sense of that word and dispels the notion that anybody can be a manager if he has some coaching skills. This book offers guidance for people who aspire to be managers and, equally importantly, it outlines why a person might *not* be suited for such a position.

The importance of a manager having the necessary control over aspects of the team other than training the players is dealt with in detail as is the necessity for the potential manager to have a minimum level of other skills such as communication ability, diplomacy and, of course, dedication among many others.

This book does not offer an easy road to management because that would be irresponsible. Stop and study are often the watchwords – don't charge into management in a rush of enthusiasm because it seems an attractive job. Look at all the pros and cons and think long and hard. How many people have taken over teams only to end up in a nightmare situation six months later because they found they were out of their depth in some particular area of management? This book tries to help people avoid that.

The GAA really needs people in charge of teams who have management skills and all the component parts of those skills. Young men playing hurling and football nowadays demand high standards of team management and will respond to that, but poor management skills invariably lead to unrest in the team and often open dissent and a consequent acrimonious falling out within different sections of the team or club or county.

People who read Tim Healy's book will learn a huge amount about how to approach GAA team management properly, with the emphasis on the word 'manage', and that is the first time they have had access to a book, based on personal experience mainly, that has provided that in the GAA.

The art of sport management encompasses a vast array of necessary qualities other than mere coaching and this book will open many previously hidden windows in that regard.

INTRODUCTION

IT was the Autumn of 2010. A number of counties were seeking new managers for their football teams. The well-known and successful manager had an idea. One of the counties in question ticked almost all his boxes. He held the place in great affection. There was plenty of football potential in the county. He had no other pressing football commitments. It would involve plenty of driving. But sure nothing is perfect and he would have time to think on those journeys. He would offer his services, entirely for altruistic reasons – money did not come into it. This would be a great challenge, something he could get his teeth into.

Contact was made and the "interview" was scheduled. All seemed to be going well with the two men directly across the table. They talked about their aspirations, their targets for the next couple of years. He spoke enthusiastically about what he believed could be achieved and how keen he was to do the job. Then the third man at the side of the table spoke up. "You don't have any coaching qualifications."

The well-known manager replied that he could coach and had coached but that as he understood it, they needed a manager. His record at club and county level spoke for itself. There had been no shortage of success. "But you don't have any formal coaching qualifications" said our friend with the coaching obsession, now warming to the topic.

The well-known manager responded by outlining his

record and pointing out, politely, that he is a manager and that he could get a coach on board without difficulty. But by now he knew that whatever else he would be doing come the Spring, he certainly would not be managing this county. He left the meeting and made the long drive home, a disappointed man and a somewhat confused one.

And the county board appointed a coach to manage their team.

There is no shortage of courses and seminars available on the topic of coaching various popular team sports. This is particularly true of the two national games of Ireland, Gaelic football and hurling. A typical example is a one-day seminar held in the new Mallow GAA complex in county Cork in March 2010.

Sponsored by the Munster council of the Gaelic Athletic Association, it was attended by 200 club coaches. The chairman of the Munster council was quoted as saying the council was currently spending €1.3m per annum on coaching and "between the colleges and the county structure we have 35 full-time coaches on the ground".

That is all very laudable and it reflects well on the GAA. However, coaching and managing teams are two different tasks. The subject of managing teams appears to have got little or no attention. Are we to assume that managing a team requires no guidance whatsoever or that it is an easier task than coaching and therefore can be done by anyone, without reference to experience, training or ability?

The legendary New York Yankees manager, Yogi Berra, was once asked the question; "what makes great managers, Yogi?" to which he replied "great players!" Maybe it is as simple as that. In support of what was probably a slightly tongue-in-cheek view, there are plenty of examples of what appear to be good, intelligent, thoughtful managers working with what might be considered less than brilliant players – and usually losing out to the big battalions with teams full of talented individuals.

Questions can be asked such as how good would Mickey Harte or Brian Cody or indeed Alex Ferguson be with a team several divisions below that occupied by their present squad. We have many examples, in all sports, of managers who have been very successful with one team and failed to achieve much with another.

But because there are also numerous examples of managers who have succeeded with limited resources and who did so consistently over time, and managers who underachieved with massive resources, it may be concluded that there is more to managing a team than simply having great players available.

So, what does it take to be a manager? What are the minimum requirements? What skills and training are needed? Why do many sports organisations, of which the GAA is just one, devote significant resources, human and financial, to coaching, while virtually ignoring the possibility that training might be required for managers of teams? In the business world, people are regularly and routinely participating in management training courses.

No business of any substance would appoint a manager at any level of the organisation without providing some degree of training and education. The world of sports places a high premium on coaching and it would appear, holds little respect for the concept that managers might require training or education before assuming their managerial role.

Without question, to manage successfully at any level it is important that the person concerned would have achieved a level of proficiency in coaching well ahead of entering management. Where the problem arises is that often it would appear that within the world of sport, the coaching experience is considered sufficient qualification to manage.

Only in sport do we see managers without training or preparation start at the top. Gaelic football and hurling regularly see retired players, without management experience or training, appointed to manage club teams, county teams and even a national team.

The Football Association of Ireland appointed Steve Staunton as manager of the national team. He had been a great player in his day, but was completely without managerial experience or training. The outcome was not one that any of those involved will view with fond memories.

Soccer offers many further examples of players moving directly from playing into management. These moves do not always end in failure but there have been very few examples of outstanding success. Even at the highest level, at least in terms of finances and resources, the Premier League in England and the corresponding European governing body, UEFA, will insist that a retiring player must acquire coaching qualifications before being allowed manage a team/club.

Again, it would appear management qualifications are not necessary. So we should not be surprised when fallout occurs and managers are said to have "lost the dressing room" or are deemed excellent coaches who lack "man-management skills".

In the aftermath of England's unsuccessful attempt at World Cup glory in South Africa, it was astonishing to hear the then highly paid football pundit, Andy Gray, from the dominant television channel, Sky Sports, offer the opinion that a change of manager was necessary and that either Alan Shearer or David Beckham should be given the job as soon as possible.

Alan Shearer has managed Newcastle United for eight games from which they required six points to avoid a costly relegation from the Premier League. They managed to get five points from a possible 24. That is Alan Shearer's total experience of management. If there is anyone out there who thinks appointing David Beckham to the England manager's job is a good idea, please keep taking the tablets.

However, this book is not about managing at the highest level. Rather, it is an attempt to offer guidance to anyone contemplating managing a club team. It is an attempt to enable them to evaluate the task and to take the decisions necessary to make their time in team management as enjoyable as possible.

That enjoyment should come from bringing about improvement, from contributing to players lives so that they feel they are in a well-run organisation making it worth their time and trouble to respond with a serious effort on behalf of the team.

We are dealing here with games at the amateur level, so these factors are important. However, the principles of sound management do not change dramatically as the manager graduates to greater challenges, whether those challenges amount to managing teams at a higher level or moving up in an organisation or to a bigger organisation. The resources are greater but as the scale increases so does the responsibility.

Although written primarily in the context of Gaelic football, the principles of managing club teams will be very similar in other team field sports. Indeed many of the principles which apply to managing your local club team will not differ significantly from those which apply at higher levels or grades.

Training for adult team management can come through the experience of working with Juvenile/Under Age teams or through gaining experience in a role such as assistant, selector, or statistician on a club management team. Others can learn the fundamentals of management in another sphere such as the business sector and apply their knowledge and experience to the benefit of their club team. That is not to say a business manager can walk into a club management role and immediately apply the same principles.

Managing is about leadership, organisation, developing the individual, turning groups into teams in the real sense of the word. The task of a business manager or the manager of a professional team will differ from that of a manager in an amateur environment. The fact that people are paid to perform a task will always bring a difference to the relationship between manager and worker, employer and employee, than what could be perceived as the more pure relationship between a manager in an amateur game and his/her players.

It could be argued that what defines the great soccer or rugby players, for example, is that they are more concerned with their performance levels and achieving success than with money. The great Gaelic footballers and Hurlers on the other hand, are primarily and pretty much exclusively motivated by the will to succeed.

My own motivation for writing this book comes from what I perceive as a concentration on preparation of qualified coaches and the contrasting total lack of concern for management training in sport. Interestingly, in the book *The Economics of Football*, (Dobson and Goddard, 2001) I found a description of how this applies in English football.

"Most football managers are ex-professional players. A playing career is the only source of previous work experience for many managers, although some enter management having previously been employed as a coach or assistant manager. There are very few managers who come into the job without some previous professional involvement in the sport. The careers of most professional players start at age 16.

"Many players therefore have only limited educational attainment, and relatively few study in further or higher education. There is a marked contrast with the typical educational attainment of managers in other business sectors. Furthermore, while the majority of managers in industry or commerce are likely to have had some formal training, only limited training opportunities exist for the football manager. The Football Association organises coaching courses, but most managers still rely primarily on their playing experience as preparation for a career in football management."

Once again, it is coaching courses all the way. Who needs management training anyway?

CHAPTER 1

SO YOU THINK YOU CAN MANAGE...

An opportunity has arisen to become manager of a team in your club, or in another club where you have been asked to step in, based on your previous success as a player, or because you have a management background in your work career. Though sport quite frequently defies reason and logic, it might not be a bad thing to rationalise any decision you wish to take with regard to becoming a team manager at club level. Ask yourself some hard questions. If you are at the point of considering the subject it is almost certain that you want to do it.

Do you believe you are sufficiently well equipped or experienced enough?

What is your understanding of the role?

What problems might arise and how will you deal with them?

It may appear over-the-top to refer to what ought to be a hobby in these terms. But it is not something you should do lightly nor is it necessarily an experience you should shy away from either. It is just better to know what you are letting yourself in for. It is better to anticipate what you will need and to be well prepared. It is better that you give yourself every chance of enjoying the experience and of achieving some level of success. So my advice then is to think and consider before you act – but do not be afraid to act.

REASONS TO MANAGE THE TEAM

1. You love the game and your playing days are over

You love the particular game in which you have been active but you have just finished playing. You would like to continue your involvement but sitting in committee meetings is not for you. Maybe it is the right time to move into management but I would advise caution. If you have not spent some time involved in management or coaching of underage/youth teams, it might be advisable to begin perhaps as an assistant, a selector or in one of the other supporting roles, with an adult team in the club, before moving into management.

That way you can get some insight into how the manager of the adult team operates. If you are keen to learn, you will definitely learn, if only how not to do it. Participate and observe and note the experiences so that when the opportunity does come to take the helm, you will have some clear ideas of what might work and what will be unlikely to work.

2. You were asked

Being asked to make the jump to management may well be flattering but it is no reason to take that step.

3. There's no one else to do it

Neither is this a good reason to take on the job. You may feel a loyalty to the club but unless you actually want the job and have some experience and preparation, it may be advisable to hold off until you are ready.

4. You believe you can improve the team

Believing you can bring something to the table is fine but it would be better if this were based on some degree of practical experience or achievement, as opposed to optimism. If you do have some experience of managing teams or managing in a business environment, you will realise that your management/support team will be critical if you are to have a chance of success. Whether you simply want the team to show improvement on previous seasons' performances, move up a grade from say junior to intermediate or from intermediate to senior or go all the way and win a championship, wanting to do it is not enough. Ensure you bring or gain some experience before committing to the task and ensure you surround yourself with people who share your objectives and bring something to the table themselves. Finally, remember only one team can win any competition in any year.

5. You are seeking personal glory or the 'expenses' appeal to you

If making a name for yourself is your objective or expenses are a factor in taking on the job, don't do it. If you prove good enough you will earn respect. If you are motivated by money, find a part-time job doing something else.

REASONS NOT TO MANAGE

1. The team is bad – God could not improve it!

The team being very bad may not actually be a reason to turn down the job. Almost any team in Gaelic football, rugby or soccer performing badly, could be improved considerably through better fitness levels, better coaching and some motivation. Assuming a fundamental level of skills within the team, the same could probably be said for most hurling teams which are struggling. Without question, the motivation levels improve as performances improve so momentum can be got fairly quickly with improved organisation and effort.

Besides, expectations around the club will be low if the team was that dismal, so you do not have a huge amount to lose and any managerial task should be a challenge. Maybe if the only way is up you should go for it!

Mike Brearley has quite a different take on whether an insider or outsider should take over an ailing team. "The more feeble the side has become, and the longer its decline has lasted, the more reason there is to import. For by then some at least of the likely candidates from within will already have been tried. Moreover, the pattern of apathy and expectation of defeat will have become entrenched."

He is talking about an extreme case here so maybe he has a point. Brearley, incidentally, is not just a former England cricket captain but a qualified psychoanalyst.

2. The club is full of factions/family interests

Many rural clubs in particular depend on a small number of families for a large proportion of their players. This has obvious advantages of togetherness but can lead to difficulties where these families have members, fathers, uncles, sometimes mothers, all over the club committee. It is not uncommon and you will know all about it if you have grown up in the club. Otherwise, be very aware of it. It is probably the most common cause of difficulty in club management.

One good friend of mine declares that the greatest joy in managing a third level colleges team is the absence of the family element. I know of clubs where the primary ambition of certain members is that their family representative makes the team. Winning a championship would come second! I was speaking with a player from a rural club who was having problems with the manager. I asked him what kind of person was his manager, "was he approachable, reasonable, what would generally be called a good man manager?"

His reply was enlightening: "he has three sons on the team – and I don't think any one of them talks to him!" Meanwhile, I have recently witnessed a situation where a championship-winning team was about to retain its manager but acquire two new replacement selectors at the club AGM.

When one name was put forward, the man's son, a prominent player on the team, announced that if his father were appointed a selector, he would not remain with the team for the coming year. The attendance at the meeting thought it was a joke – until it became clear that the player was serious – and another selector was chosen. That must have made for a very interesting breakfast table!

3. Previous brilliant manager is a hard act to follow

Following a really good person in any role in life has disadvantages. Realise you will be compared to a successful or charismatic predecessor. If you are strong enough of character to put up with that, and everything else being ok, take the job. If it bothers you, say no.

4. Too much time required

Time is a requirement in managing any club team. Be aware that you will need to make a serious commitment. If you have other involvements, if you have heavy work or family demands, do not take on the job. It has been said in recent years that the time required for success at the higher levels in Gaelic football is such that only teachers and students need apply. This may not be completely true, but it is not far off the mark. Depending on what grade you play in, club competition can also be extremely competitive and therefore demanding of time. Unless you know you will be available pretty much all the time do not create an impossible situation for yourself. Of course there will be times when you cannot make a training session because of a family event or through work related travel or such. This is where your management team is critical. You will need to create a situation where in such an event you are not actually missed.

5. Insufficient experience

This, I believe is a good reason not to take on the job. To which some will respond by asking how can you get experience if you keep turning down jobs or not seeking them in the first place. The best way to prepare for a managerial job is to start out coaching youngsters. Inevitably you will find yourself managing a team at that level. Alternatively, become involved in a secondary role with an adult team. Become an assistant manager or a selector or commit to doing stats for a team. In the latter scenario, say as a selector, you will have the advantage of not having to make the hard decisions or at least not being held responsible for them. If you have the ambition to manage, then observe and learn as you go on. Think about issues that arise over the course of the season. Consider how they were addressed and how you might have gone about dealing with these matters. Ultimately, to develop the necessary understanding of the game, you should gain experience coaching.

SUMMARY

1. *Gain experience before taking on the management of an adult team. This can be done through first working with under age teams and/or in a support role with a senior manager.*

2. *Consider all the known facts before committing.*

3. *Take on the job for the right reasons.*

4. *Before agreeing to start, make sure you can give the job the time and attention it requires.*

5. *Become a coach first, and then a manager.*

CHAPTER 2

THE MANAGEMENT TEAM

"Surround yourself with people strong enough to change your mind." **John Wooden**

TITLE - MANAGER OR COACH

There is always an element of overlap between managing and coaching. It can also be confusing in that the role of manager in one sport can be pretty much identical to the role of coach in another. Elsewhere, I quote from Mike Brearley, the former Middlesex and England cricket captain's seminal work *The Art of Captaincy*. Clearly the role of captain of a cricket team is on a par with that of player-manager in other sports such as soccer. The critical decisions relating to team selection, setting out the field (positioning of fielders etc), the order in which players will either bowl or bat, are just some of the responsibilities of the cricket captain.

In hockey, at least at the more advanced levels, it appears the manager and coach have a more clearly defined division of responsibilities, with coaching, playing strategy, tactics, motivation and team selection, all the prerogative of the coach.

The managers, or at least the ones with whom I spoke, tend to take care of putting in place the entire management team, including the coach, and dealing with all logistical arrangements while maintaining an overview to ensure the relationship and inter-action between coach and players is good.

Video analysis is the norm among the better clubs with every game video recorded and analysed by a specific member of management. Clubs playing somewhere below the very top levels may involve the team captain in the selection process. Without the sophisticated video analysis equipment, they will frequently video games and will have some basic stats measured during each game, for use at half-time and in the subsequent performance review. In rugby, at the highest level, the man in charge is described as the coach. Once again though, his role appears to be quite similar to that of manager at a top Gaelic football team. Club rugby at the basic levels, will have a manager who is largely responsible for logistics, while the head coach is the decision maker in terms of team matters, and to all intents and purposes, he fulfils a role similar to the manager of a Gaelic or soccer team. Because there is such a difference of approach needed between forward play and back play in rugby, the assistant coach is also very important as he will be chosen based on the head coach's area of expertise to ensure he complements the head coach, i.e. if the head coach is a forwards coach, the assistant coach will be a backs coach and vice-versa.

Additionally, virtually all club rugby teams will have a conditioning coach who will work with the squad pre-season and throughout the season, typically once a week during the playing season. Video analysis is in common usage among rugby teams and a manager/coach taking over a team would be well advised to ensure games are recorded for analysis if such an arrangement is not already in place.

The top clubs will video every game and as with hockey clubs, they will most likely have a single person charged with responsibility for recording as well as analysis of games and significantly, they will have access to video analysis equipment. Also, the top clubs in amateur rugby tend to have a physiotherapist and usually a doctor in attendance at all games. In both rugby and hockey it tends to be a matter of resources. While we are dealing with amateur sports, the further up the ladder one looks, the better the equipment and the more comprehensive the management team and support team.

A common management structure in amateur soccer would see a manager, an assistant manager, a coach and a goalkeeping coach. Physiotherapists are sometimes made available at training while video analysis is less used than in other sports such as rugby, hockey, hurling and Gaelic football. The responsibility for the team rests with the manager while the other members of management are there to support him/her.

The assistant manager will act in a similar manner to a selector in Gaelic games while the coach will sometimes have responsibility for physical preparation as well as working on individual skills and most importantly on dead ball situations. The better run clubs or perhaps the clubs with greater resources will have a separate person responsible for fitness and conditioning. The coach will drill the team in defending corners and free kicks as well as in the execution of both. He will work closely with the manager, carrying out his instructions in terms of improving players and team.

The AFL Aussie Rules manual on coaching tends to give the coach a very wide-ranging set of responsibilities. The coach is said to be expected to fill a number of roles including: Manager, Leader, Teacher, Selector, Communicator, Psychologist, Public Relations Expert, Student and Sports Trainer.

It is reasonable to state that the Australians are certainly getting value for money if their coach can meet all of these requirements. It is also fair to point out that in most team sports, the manager would not, and could not, be expected to fulfil all of these tasks. Whatever the title, the intention of this book is to deal with the act of managing and all that this entails in the context of an amateur sports team, at club level.

CHARACTERISTICS OF THE MANAGEMENT TEAM

Before addressing the more mundane aspects of the management team, its functions and the tasks it must be capable of carrying out, it might be useful to consider the more cerebral perspective – what kind of people should you bring on board? What kind of personalities do you want? Should they be people who agree with you 100 per cent all the time? Should they be people who challenge you all the time?

Ian McGeechan (*Lion Man – The Autobiography*) refers to this when he says: *"But if you are on the same wavelength, do you also have to like the people in your coaching group? What is far more important is honesty. I have worked with people who are known as spiky characters – Jim Telfer and Shaun Edwards come to mind. But from that honesty comes respect, and the most important thing is respect for differences of opinion."*

Interestingly, the most successful Gaelic football manager of recent times, Mickey Harte of Tyrone, sings from an almost identical hymn-sheet when speaking of the need to respect people's differences.

The legendary UCLA basketball coach, John Wooden, says: "Surround yourself with people strong enough to change your mind"

An eminent rugby man for whom I have great respect once described the Irish rugby team under successive and quite different management regimes. The first manager, he said, wanted a backroom team in which nobody could possibly offer a threat to him. His successor wanted the best possible people available in all the key roles. He was not concerned about threats but about building a better organisation. The team results, not surprisingly, reflect this difference of approach.

Without any question, it is advisable to get the best possible people for the various management roles. Also, my advice would be not to underestimate the importance of any role. For example, while you may have people on administration duties or looking after statistics or kit, dealing with tasks which are not directly concerned with team selection or performance, it is not a bad idea to let them express their views and observations.

The fact that they are part of the management team, whatever their role, ought to entitle them to have the ear of the manager, should any matter directly or not directly involving their duties cause them to feel the need to express a concern or an opinion. Very often, someone who is not as close to a particular issue may see, or indeed hear, something which those in the thick of it have not noticed.

I learned a long time ago that it can pay to let everyone express their opinion, not just the ones who shout loudest. I recall a committee meeting many years ago when a weekly club lottery was the main topic of discussion. The lottery was held in the local pub (there being no clubhouse) every Sunday night.

The two people who ran the lottery were, for different reasons, encountering difficulty with Sundays and the thrust of the discussion was about getting someone else who would be available consistently on Sunday nights or a group of people who could perform the job on a rota basis.

This was proving difficult as person after person had some problem which prevented them volunteering. I am ashamed to say that the debate went on for quite some time and just as it seemed to be fizzling out, no nearer to a solution, the quietest person in the room made his only intervention with the simple suggestion; "why don't we move it to Monday nights?" It is called "lateral thinking." Problem solved. Lesson learned.

FUNCTIONS OF THE MANAGEMENT TEAM

Having been appointed manager, your first task before you even contemplate what players you will have, is what management structure will be required. There was a time when management personnel as applied to Gaelic football and hurling, whether at representative level or at club level, consisted of the manager and either 2 or 4 selectors.

You will need selectors, depending on your knowledge of the team you are about to manage. If, for example, you are an outsider, asked to come in and shake up an underachieving team, you will certainly need inside help. Ideally, you should have two selectors with some knowledge of the team's recent performances. Within your own club, it is also advisable to have selectors or an assistant whom you should nominate.

Often, there will be a precedent whereby the chairman or the committee decides who should fill these roles. It is of critical importance to you that you get along with these individuals so unless you are being offered people with whom there already exists mutual respect, make sure their appointment is your call, with the chairman or Committee simply rubber stamping their appointment.

To all intents and purposes, in Gaelic games, your selectors are your assistant managers. You will require a coach and you will need a physical trainer. Ideally, you should have someone looking after gear and equipment and someone who is essentially secretary to the team management. You will also need someone doing statistics.

The variations in management structure for other team games have already been mentioned. A summary might look something like this:

GAELIC GAMES	SOCCER	HOCKEY	RUGBY
1. Manager	Manager	Head Coach	Head Coach
2. Two Selectors	Assistant Manager	Manager (Admin)	Assistant Coach
3. Coach	Coach	Fitness Expert	Manager (Admin)
4. Trainer	Goalkeeping Coach	Video Analyst	Conditioning Expert
5. Secretary	Conditioning Expert	Sports Psychologist	Video Analyst
6. Gear/Kit person	Physio	Goalkeeping Coach	Kicking Coach
7. Statistician	-	Physio	Physio
8. Physio	-	-	Team Doctor

No one list of managerial roles will apply to every club. For example, most soccer or hockey clubs will have more than one team, often several. Almost certainly, the goalkeeping coach will look after all goalkeepers from all the club teams. A rugby club will have several teams and one kicking coach will serve all the teams. I have already outlined how better resourced clubs, particularly in rugby and hockey will tend to have a bigger management team than the more humble club.

If you are starting out, do not expect limitless resources or equipment at the outset. It is necessary to work within the parameters appropriate to the club's position or ranking.

Under the above heading 'Gaelic Games', the management team appears to make a total of up to nine people. Not necessarily. In some sports, the manager, where he/she is suitably qualified, may double as coach. The manager should have trained and operated as a coach so as to develop a greater understanding of the game. He/she may double up as manager and coach but the workload may be better spread if a separate person can concentrate on the coaching role, working closely with the manager.

Alternatively, a selector or assistant manager may double as coach or as physical trainer. The other selector could then become responsible for the secretarial function and/or gear/kit. Or a selector or the secretary could look after stats, although my own preference is for a separate person on stats so they can concentrate on what is happening during the game, without interruption.

In relation to the role of physiotherapist, some clubs across the sports tend to have a qualified person in attendance at training on a specific night each week. Where funds allow and where the requirement is considered valid, the person may be in attendance on a second night. Where funds are scarce, which applies in the majority of cases, the club may have an arrangement to send players to a particular physiotherapist who will treat players at his/her clinic rather than attend the club's training venue.

Sports psychology is becoming increasingly prominent in professional sport and in representative team sport such as inter-county hurling or football. However, I found few examples of regular club teams in any codes, having access to a sports psychologist on a regular basis. It may be that a particular hockey club had such access because the professional in question had an interest in the sport and the club. Sports psychology is addressed elsewhere in this book.

You should look at the above list of functions and your first task as manager is to allocate responsibilities among the people you have chosen to be your management team. You will, of course, have started from the position of needing the above listed tasks and responsibilities distributed, and you will have chosen your management team with that in mind.

What are the responsibilities and background requirements for the various tasks? Which tasks can be doubled up? Can a manager also coach? Can the coach be a physical trainer? Etc, etc. The following is an outline of the requirements for some of the essential management roles.

SELECTOR/ASSISTANT MANAGER

As the word suggests, the selector is responsible for contributing to team selection. Consequently, this person needs to be available and present at training sessions, practice games and all competitive games. This should be someone whose opinions on the subject, you trust. They may be, but do not have to be ex-players. One of the best selectors I ever worked with was, by his own admission, pretty harmless as a player. As a result, he lacked credibility with some of the people who knew-it-all, but I found him thoughtful, insightful and always constructive and in general, a huge help.

He may not have played at a high level but he was a student of Gaelic football at all levels and ideally suited to selecting teams. The manager and selectors, having chosen their team, must also make plans for all eventualities which may arise during a game – in particular a championship game. It is a worthwhile practice, on such occasions to conduct a what-if exercise. What if our full back is injured?

What if our key midfielder or our free kicker is injured, or worse still, red carded? I liked to run through the team when it had been selected and make a mental list of the options available should any of the starting line-up be injured, in the course of a game. Needless to say, one hopes the lessons and preaching about discipline lead to a clean slate in terms of sendings off. But, you know it can happen. If you need to play with a one-man disadvantage, what tactics will you employ.

In Gaelic games, where you find yourself a man down, you may be assured, the opposition will almost certainly park the spare man around their half back line or even between the full and half back lines. Your players need to ensure they avoid panic and refrain from kicking ball straight into the spare man's position. How often it happens. These are scenarios in which a selector can bring his knowledge and experience to provide advice to the manager.

So, in summary, the main responsibilities of the selector are helping to pick the team, helping to make beneficial changes, either by a positional switch or by introducing a substitute, making tactical suggestions in advance of a game or as a game unfolds, helping the manager in all of these areas and sometimes helping in assessing the opposition before important games.

So the qualifications for becoming a selector are or should be knowledge of the game and an ability to offer judgement on players. The role of assistant manager (or in rugby, assistant coach) will be quite similar. Such a person will also deputise for the manager in the event of his/her absence at any time during the season.

PHYSICAL TRAINER - FITNESS OR CONDITIONING EXPERT

There was a time when the trainer and manager were one and the same thing. Most football people in Kerry will still refer to a manager as "training a team". The legendary Dr Eamon O'Sullivan was almost always referred to as "Kerry team trainer". The trainer was the main man who trained the team, picked the team, and advised on tactics or playing systems in so far as they applied or were discernable.

In recent times the word "training" is taken to apply only to physical preparation and conditioning. The trainer's role is to deliver a fit team in time for the championship or principle competition and to see that fitness levels are maintained over the season. One of the common features of managing in business, industry, or sports is that the manager does not necessarily have to know everything about each facet of the task, physical preparation of the team being the case in point. However, he/she does need to avail of the services of someone who is properly qualified to carry out that function. This is not as easy as it may seem.

Fitness has become a science and serious damage can be done by putting a squad of players in the charge of a trainer who is not up to the task. My father had a great phrase to describe a particular type of person "it's not that he knows nothing, he just knows a lot of things that ain't so". Never was that description more appropriate than in looking at potential trainers.

Essentially, you will need to do your research, seek advice, and make sure your trainer does not come into the category of self appointed experts who know a lot that ain't so. Therefore thought needs to be given to what is required. I would advise anyone going into team management to go and to speak with people who are involved in the physical preparation of teams.

Speak to people, not necessarily with a view to having them become your trainer but to get a feel for what is required and where you might start the search. I am assuming you will need to appoint a trainer either because there is a new management team taking over or because the previous trainer was not performing or simply not up to it.

If the latter is believed to be the case, it is possible the previous trainer was not supported by previous management. If he/she saw their function as turning up and implementing a training programme but found management did not ensure full attendance at sessions, then a perceived lack of fitness in the team may well be attributable to management failings rather than the trainer.

Depending on the level at which the team is competing, the training programme may need to include gym work, weight training, regular fitness work on the field. The appointed trainer will have to advise on the most appropriate course, taking into account such factors as availability of players on given nights, availability of facilities etc.

COACH

Collins dictionary defines a coach as: "a trainer or instructor" or "a tutor who prepares students for examination". I found the origin of the word coach fascinating – Collins again "from Hungarian kocsi szekér - wagon of Kocs, village in Hungary where first coaches were made: in the sense to teach, probably from the idea that the instructor carried his pupils". I have heard of a player being credited with carrying a team – but never have I heard of a human coach so described.

The coach is a critical member of management. As a

direct result of the emphasis on coaching courses, every club has its share of qualified coaches these days. Accredited courses are run throughout the winter months in every region and across the various codes/sports. Coaching officers have been put in place by county boards and by national governing bodies in soccer and rugby nationally and internationally. Books, DVDs and manuals are readily available. There cannot be a GAA club in existence where members have not completed basic courses such as foundation and level 1 coaching courses.

The foundation courses are a requirement for anyone wishing to take charge of an underage team. National rugby associations (Foundation through to Level 3) and soccer governing bodies such as The Football Association of Ireland (introductory through to UEFA Pro Licence) also provide coaching courses from the basic introductory levels to the elite levels which are a prerequisite for coaching the top teams.

Children from seven or eight years of age are attending Saturday morning coaching sessions. They are being coached after school and on the ubiquitous summer camps. Most major sports are also being coached within the school structure. Therefore it would be logical to assume the basics do not need to be drilled into the group of young adults you have just inherited.

You may like to imagine that coaching will involve devising a tactical plan and getting the players used to it. In implementing your carefully thought out plan, you may assume your players will perform fundamental skills, they will never commit a technical foul such as, in Gaelic football, picking a ball directly from the ground (this is within the rules in ladies football) or throwing a ball instead of hand-passing correctly. In soccer they will be familiar with the offside rule and rarely transgress. In rugby, they will have basic handling and kicking skills, and so on.

Notwithstanding such a proliferation of coaches and coaching sessions, making any of the aforementioned assumptions is the road to ruin. Because the game of Gaelic football has evolved so that hand-passing dominates over the kicked pass, the standard of kicking has diminished. It is not uncommon to see an inter-county player, on the biggest stage, kick a ball 25 or 30 metres directly to an opponent.

Quite frequently, the standard of hand-passing also leaves a lot to be desired. It is said that one of the foreign legion of rugby coaches, on coming to Ireland in recent years, found players at senior representative levels who wanted to devise intricate passing moves but who were a long way from perfect in performing basic passing at speed and under pressure. Incidentally, this was said of a professional team so take nothing for granted.

In describing the All Ireland Club Final 2010 where St.Galls of Antrim beat Kilmurray-Ibrickane from Clare, Páidí Ó Sé (*Sunday Independent*, 21st March 2010) had this to say about the standard of play: *"Neither team had much in the way of real football talent, which is perhaps the reason they insisted on playing the short game, at which they were a long way from being masters. I saw only two players who could kick a ball, the St Galls midfielder, Aodhan Gallagher and their wing-forward, Simon Downes".*

Páidí went on to make an interesting observation about the short (hand-passing dominated) game. *"Tyrone are the masters of the short game, but it must never be forgotten that they spend many, many hours on the practice pitch drilling themselves on the moves. It is absurd for other teams lacking the talent and the appetite for hard work that Tyrone possess, to try to imitate the style. It ends up in an inglorious muddle".*

Now, whether or not you are a fan of Páidí Ó Sé, and after that article he might struggle for fans in west Belfast or Quilty, his criticism of this specific game is echoed in many reports and critiques of Gaelic football in the 21st century.

Consequently, the coach will be required to drill the team in the basic skills of the game. The coach should have a variety of drills which can be deployed to improve skills such as kicking, passing, scoring and tackling. A good coach will also be able to help individuals with aspects of their game which need attention, such as turning over ball too easily, kicking for scores from bad positions or perhaps not having a clear idea of how to play in their chosen position.

Referring specifically to Gaelic football and hurling, this is where the roles of coach and manager will overlap (assuming they are not one and the same person). The coach should ideally be working to help develop players for a game-plan devised by the manager. In summary, the trainer is responsible for fitness, the coach for skills. However, as manager it is ultimately your call as to the approach to physical fitness and the approach to coaching for improvement in individuals and in the team. The coach, no more than the trainer, should be implementing your plans. (Further reference to coaching team rather than individuals, using video and stats, is made in a later paragraph headed 'statistician'.)

As already mentioned, a club team in rugby will, of necessity, have different coaches for the backs and forwards, usually one of these being the head coach, who is effectively the equivalent of a GAA or soccer manager.

GEAR/KIT PERSON

One among the management team will take responsibility for gear. This ought to include knowing and communicating to the squad, what gear is available and what is required of them in this respect. e.g. the club shorts and socks must be purchased, from the club secretary, from a club shop or from a particular sports shop in the area. Tracksuits (hurleys and helmets for hurling teams) are available through whatever channel and are either optional or necessary, depending on what has been agreed within the panel or perhaps as a general rule of the club.

Gear such as team shirts/jerseys will have to be laundered and the kit person should have an arrangement in place, approved by the club management. This person must also take responsibility for whatever may be required to help preparation of the team, such as (whichever is appropriate) balls, cones, poles, or any other equipment from tackle bags to SAC (speed, agility, quickness) sets of mini hurdles etc.

STATISTICIAN

Stats have become popular in recent times, especially in Gaelic football. As managers have sought to get an edge, a more scientific approach has been applied. Video analysis is used by all county teams. The top rugby teams such as Munster and Leinster have a full-time person on video analysis.

USE OF VIDEO ANALYSIS

Nowadays, particularly after big games such as All Ireland finals, we read that one team hand-passed the ball so many times, completing X per cent of the attempted passes while the opposition completed Y per cent of their kicked pass attempts. During international football tournaments such as the World Cup finals, commentators are fed data from constant analysis of how many passes a player has attempted and completed, how many shots on/off target, even how many metres a player has run during his time on the field. The levels of sophistication to which video analysis has been taken are quite extraordinary.

Ian McGeechan describes the scene on the most recent Lions tour of South Africa. *"Another feature of the tour was the decision that every player should have a laptop, appropriately coloured red. Rhys Long and Rhodi Brown, the analysts, set up a server with 32 ports in it, so the players could come up to the team room with their computers, plug in and download the information and analysis from the server. For example, each individual could click on one game, and find statistics to assess his performance and his involvement in attack and defence. Gethin Jenkins, for example, could assess himself in the scrum, line-out, handling and tackling. He could actually rerun his own performance, so that in around three minutes he could watch a potted version of his own game."*

If you are managing a club team in Gaelic games or soccer and fortunate enough to be in a club where the suitable video analysis equipment has been purchased and someone has been trained to use it, then you are ahead of nearly everyone else. If such equipment is light years away, do not despair. The most basic form of analysis can still be carried out, to the benefit of the team and at little or no cost.

Hockey and rugby clubs appear better equipped in terms of video analysis and consequently they make greater more frequent use of this highly valuable tool. I qualify this by adding that it tends to depend on the level at which the hockey or rugby club is competing.

Firstly, the alternative route that has some costs and which assumes you are without sophisticated video analysis equipment: get someone in the club or near the club to video a game, early in the year. It can be a league game or a friendly/challenge match. Take the DVD and along with your fellow management members look at it and make notes on the incidents which exemplified good and bad decision-making, or use of individual skills or aspects of your team's play. Arrange to bring the team together to view the dvd. Take this exercise seriously.

Do not allow access to anyone other than squad members and team management. Team management may decide to show only half the game or to fast forward some segments from which not much new information can be taken. This would help to reduce boredom and to shorten the time required for this exercise. Before showing the video, outline from your notes the list of good and bad examples of play, and the sequence in which they will be seen, asking the players to watch for these.

You may want to stop the dvd at particular moments to make points that can be easily understood as the examples are there for all to see. This is a very good way to demonstrate to a player or to a group of players, how improvement is necessary and how it can be brought about. It is infinitely more effective than telling a player on the training ground, even one-to-one, what he has done wrong. Seeing it takes away any doubts and the basis for improvement has to be recognition that there is a problem in the first place.

You would be surprised at how reluctant some people can be to acknowledge they were less than perfect in the game on Sunday. It is also true that the player with an inclination to learn, the good student of the game, will readily accept constructive criticism when it is presented properly, especially when he/she can see his/her own performance on dvd.

It is not necessary to video every game played. However, having identified areas for improvement, you should be working with the coach to improve these aspects of team and individual play. A second video a few months later, ideally some weeks before the championship or primary competition, should enable everyone to take stock of progress since the initial game.

If you are making progress through the competitions, you may wish to repeat this exercise more frequently. At that stage you are seeking to make further improvements but also to encourage players, to bolster confidence by showing aspects of play that have improved. On that note, while the initial video is being used to highlight deficiencies make a point of also highlighting satisfactory aspects of the play.

Players will respond to praise and there is no better way to illustrate something positive you want to see repeated through the season, than to show it being done by your own player(s) on screen. And video analysis, even of the most basic kind, has application in any team sport. The video, in this context, has been described as the most instructive device imaginable.

Many club rugby teams now video every game they play. Like many hockey teams they have a member of the management team whose responsibility is to see that all games are recorded and analysed. It depends on resources and on whether you think there is something to be gained from going to this level. I have outlined the most rudimentary use of videos by an amateur club. My thinking is influenced not only by cost but by the sheer time it takes to study videos and extract the relevant points, good and bad. If the software is available to enable detailed analysis, well and good, but even without that, useful, if fairly simple analysis and learning can still be derived from videos of occasional games.

CHEAP AND EFFECTIVE STATS

At no cost, you can get useful statistics every time you play. Decide what exactly you wish to measure, devise a simple sheet for recording details during a game and have someone - your statistician or stats person record the incidents as they occur.

Examples of aspects of play (in Gaelic football) which you might deem important are:

a) Frees committed.
b) Kick-outs won and lost at either end.
c) Balls turned over to opposition.
d) Possession recovered.
e) Shots sent wide, chances wasted.
f) Kicks dropping short to goalkeeper.

For different sports, this will vary. In rugby you will want information on line-outs, scrums, mauls, ball retention, territory gained etc. In hockey or soccer or basketball the elements measured will again be a little different but suffice to say, it is the key elements which you will want to measure. I contend that any team ball game can be broken down to what a team does: a) when they have the ball and: b) when the opposition has the ball. Most analysis will confirm that.

It may be measuring performance at set pieces in soccer or hockey while possession and turnovers will be a big feature in basketball. The manager and coach should decide which features they want measured and create a simple one-page form on which these elements of play may be recorded.

Scores and scorers will, of course, be recorded. You may wish to add other requirements such as the number of times during a game you managed to get the ball inside the oppositions 45m or 20m line and the percentage scores to chances created. Do not make it too complicated. Focus on a few key basics like possession from kick-outs, ball turned over and ball recovery.

All you require is a hand-held clipboard with a list of your team, by number on a backup sheet, with some additional sheets which have the above elements boxed off. Your statistician writes the number of the player who gave the ball away, committed the foul etc. At the end of a game, or more appropriately at half-time or at the review meeting, you are able to tell how many fouls were committed and by whom. You are able to tell who recovered ball and who gave it away – and how often. Those fairly basic facts can be hugely helpful in trying to bring about change and improvement.

These statistics, costing nothing, just the undivided attention of one person cataloguing them, can help you set goals and address areas where the greatest improvement must be made. I would say the two most important factors are the quality and understanding of the person taking these stats/notes and the manner in which you analyse the data and follow up.

While statistics may be analysed at leisure after a game, they can sometimes be of great benefit for half-time analysis. In the heat of the moment it is not always possible to spot a trend in a game, such as excessive fouling, perhaps by a particular team member. A good stats person, looking at the appropriate aspects of the play will highlight key factors which can then be addressed in the half-time talk.

If you believe statistics can be of benefit, an improved option might be to use more than one person. There have been examples of stats teams being deployed to measure virtually every movement by every player, but from talking with people who work in this area at inter-county level and from my own experience, this is overkill.

In 2010 Waterford hurlers had a team of 12 people working on a computer based programme to monitor the performances of the players on the field. Eight of this stats team had hand-held devices linked to a main computer. They monitored two players each with one taking just the goalkeeper.

The cost of the system was €16,500. Of this amount, €3,000 was provided by the supporters club but those directly involved, quite remarkably, put their own money into the venture. The people who put it in place were volunteers who believed it was the ultimate system which provided instant feedback and enabled the manager to take corrective action at the earliest possible moment. This appeared to work up to a point.

The point was when the Waterford team manager chose to ignore the information at half-time in the All Ireland semi-final, a game which Waterford ultimately lost to Tipperary. The fallout was not nice, with the leaders of the voluntary team claiming the manager never even looked at the half-time data and effectively blamed that action or inaction for their team's defeat. The entire episode does show the lengths to which some people are prepared to go in terms of committing their time and money to a cause.

A more conservative, but effective method used by some county teams is the use of up to four people. Bypassing technology, they simply have two people watching the opposition, one calling the information and one noting it, with a similar exercise underway for their own team. The person or persons doing the calling cannot get involved in following the game as a regular spectator or supporter would. They must simply spot every incident which requires noting and call it to the note-taker alongside.

Most club teams that I have seen using basic stats, do so from the perspective of their own team. I like the idea of also getting detail on the actions of the opposition players. Anything that helps confirm where the threat arises or where an opponent's weakness presents an opportunity is worth considering. From your perspective as a manager of a club team, you need to establish what resources are available. It may not be too difficult to get your team of up to four working as described above. The best way to experiment is to try this or any similar idea out during less important games early in the season. You will soon establish how worthwhile the exercise may prove.

A reason to strongly recommend both use of statistics and the videoing of games is that they overcome another frequent problem. Almost every coach on a coaching course is looking for drills – new drills, so much so that good coaching is often deemed synonymous with having a wide variety of drills. However, a player can improve his basic skills such as kicking, hand-passing, catching overhead, tackling, blocking, etc. and still play poorly in games.

Until the coaching helps with more team-related issues such as defending as a team, movement of ball to forwards, shot options being taken, movement off the ball etc., then the improvements to which you aspire will not happen. The statistics and the use of video as described will help you. In addition, it is important that the team plays games. It's a bit like the question "what do we get good at by lapping a field every night?" Answer: lapping a field. Well, what do we get good at by playing more games (while bringing the learning from stats and videos on to the field)? The answer should be: we get good at playing games. An interesting observation I recently read was that with 30 players training, (this would be 22 in soccer) when a practice game is being set up, there is a tendency to pick the first choice backs on one team to mark the first choice forwards on the other.

The point being made was that it is worthwhile putting the first 15 on one team regardless of the relative strength of the reserves, as the first choice players need to play together and would benefit from playing together as often as possible. The obvious downside to this suggestion is that the first team may be so much better than the second that the ball is permanently in one half of the field, with no benefit to half those present.

MEASURING

In dealing with stats and how to use them, it might be appropriate to look at other opportunities to measure. Indeed, stats are simply a measurement of some elements of the team's play. As with all measurements of this nature, they are taken repeatedly over a period, to assess improvement. As the other measurements described here require a certain amount of work and organisation, it might be best to have the stats person also be responsible for these and their subsequent monitoring.

Introducing dietary advice early on is addressed elsewhere in this book. There are at least two measurements which can be taken at this early stage. Each player can be weighed. Some will lack bulk and size and may need gym work (a prescribed weights programme) to assist them become stronger. Others will be overweight and will need to avail of the dietary advice combined with the training regime. A second measurement is BMI or body mass index. It is an easily and frequently used simple calculation to indicate whether a person is over or under weight. The person advising on dietary matters will be able to explain and advise on BMI measuring and monitoring.

The "Beep Test" or "Bleep Test" is a commonly used test to assess cardiovascular fitness. Your trainer should know how to carry out this test and should have access to the necessary CD/soundtrack. If you have no information on either BMI testing or Beep Testing, you will get all the detail you need in 15 minutes on the internet.

The point about measuring is that you are monitoring progress under various headings. You will have records showing progress and you will have created awareness among the players that they will be measured so that lack of progress or improvement will become obvious. Checking and recording weights and BMI measurements at the outset can be followed up with repeats of these tests at fixed intervals, say two months and again four months from the initial tests.

Similarly the initial beep test will create an acute awareness of where players are in general fitness terms and in comparison to each other. Subjecting players to beep tests every two months will give you information and keep them on their toes. The very fact that they know these tests are being carried out will help you in your own efforts. There will be the occasional excuse such as a player being unwell or recovering from a virus at the time of the test. As with all of these ideas, you must not let test results over-rule common sense. You may give a player the benefit of the doubt once but if you both know the test will be repeated before long, the wool cannot be pulled over your eyes forever.

A few words of caution. I came across a situation where a player (quite a decent footballer) who tended to be a little on the chubby side was also extremely self-conscious about his weight. Being weighed in front of a bunch of joking teammates after training was an enormous ordeal.

Weigh people individually with just one management member doing the weighing and recording in a private room in some part of the training facility. You are trying to use this as a means of getting people to improve. It is not an occasion for anyone to be embarrassed or subjected to unwelcome comments.

SUMMARY

1. *Stats can be produced the expensive sophisticated way*

2. *Videos / dvds are relatively inexpensive and can be most useful coaching tools, for both individual and team coaching*

3. *Whatever the system, interpreting the statistics meaningfully is key to their usefulness*

4. *Where possible use regular measurement to gauge progress and to provide feedback to the players*

MANAGER

The role of the football manager is comprehensively described in *The Economics of Football* (Dobson and Goddard). That book draws on the teaching and writing of Henry Mintzberg, the renowned Canadian academic and author on the subjects of business and management. It describes the three broad management functions as outlined by Mintzberg. These are interpersonal relations which incorporates leadership and motivation, information processing and decision making and their role in football management is described as follows:

"The way in which a football manager treats his players can affect not only the performance of the individual player, but also the performance of the team. In the information-processing role the manager will use match reports and videos to analyse and assess the performance of players, in order to formulate plans and strategies. It is also likely that the manager will delegate responsibility, by employing coaches and scouts, to help disseminate information. Finally, the decision making role involves determining the organisation of the team (team formation) and the role of individual players both before and during the game (pre-match and half-time team talk and strategic substitutions). The manager's ability to respond rapidly to situations such as a player suffering a loss of form or an injury can of course make all the difference between the team achieving success or failure."

Chambers Dictionary rather quaintly defines a manager as: "one who organises other people's doings".

Collins, on the other hand, has a more prosaic definition of the word manage: "to be in charge".

That's it in simple English. If you are the manager, you are in charge. Your management team will work with you and to you. Use whatever cliché you like, such as "the buck stops with you". It is important that you have a clear idea of how you expect things to work and that you communicate that to everyone from the very beginning of your time in charge. The management team you have put in place must function like a team. Any disharmony or lack of support for each other will quickly register with players and will not help you in your efforts to turn the group into a well-functioning team.

The following are some of the logistical issues you will need to address at the very outset. By doing so, you avoid problems later. Many of these points may seem basic but it is never any harm to be organised, to ensure you control the things you can control and to ensure there are no unpleasant surprises or panic stations all because someone forgot to make an arrangement or thought someone else was dealing with the matter. As the manager you are trying to create the impression of organisation and attention to detail which will make life less difficult for everyone, as the season progresses.

First impressions are very important. The impression you create should be one of competence which inspires confidence. If you have got your management team in place, and the lines of responsibility clarified, it becomes much easier to address the players with confidence.

I recall in the nineties talking to a coach appointed by Leinster Council of the GAA. His role was to visit clubs, to assess needs and to arrange coaching courses and help put coaches in place so the clubs became self sufficient. An inter-county player himself, he talked about the number of inter-county players he would meet in the course of his work, who would tell him they had never had a one-to-one conversation with the manager of the county team of which they were a part.

While we might like to think that aspect of the manager/player relationship has changed, all the evidence suggests it has not. A much more recent example is a young player of my acquaintance who spent 2008 on a senior county panel, much of the year on the starting fifteen. His manager never spoke to him once in the entire year. And this was a manager drafted in from another county where he had established some reputation managing their team.

If managing amounts to "organising other people's doings", in this case it is organising the management team and the playing squad so that everyone is clear as to what is required, on the agreed objectives and on how you propose, as a team, to set about achieving those objectives.

In this context, the early days of your management tenure are critical. You will need to ensure your management team is clear on what is and what is not important, on how responsibilities are to be allocated and on how communication will work.

The management team will have to be clear on who is responsible for every facet of your organisation.

1. Who will ensure the changing room or clubhouse is open in time for training sessions or games?

2. Who is responsible for equipment such as footballs, bibs, cones, poles or any other equipment?

3. Who will ensure the hot water system is turned on in time, so there are hot showers available after the session?

4. Who will turn on/off the floodlights?

5. If you are travelling to away games, do you require a bus? Who will arrange this and arrange a payment method for the supplier?

6. Have you agreed with club management what costs can be incurred?

7. Have you agreed which nights are available to your particular team, if playing facilities or dressing room space are limited?

8. If you are restricted for space, is there another venue nearby to which you have access when required?

9. Is there a facility within the club to hold meetings and maybe look at a video of a game? If not, where may you go, is there a cost and is that cleared in advance with club management?

When you have established the answers to all of these questions, ensure the person responsible for each task is quite clear about that responsibility, with no misunderstandings.

Use checklists. Don't be afraid to put it in writing. Copy your management team with the checklists. You arrange a challenge game. The two teams are ready to go onto the field when someone asks, who will referee the game? If your checklist for challenge/friendly games includes everything from opening grounds and clubhouse to putting up nets and pitch-side flags, it will also include "arrange referee" and another possible problem of omission will be avoided.

I once served on a club committee whose meetings were held in a room upstairs in a local public house. The room was available free of charge to anyone who reserved it in time. I remember arriving to meetings on several occasions only to find the club secretary had assumed the room would be free ("because it was always free on that night of the week") only to find the room was occupied by another group. One phone call could have saved a whole committee unnecessary inconvenience. Mind you, a semi-competent secretary may have been an alternative solution.

In Gaelic games, clearly there have been serious breakdowns in the manager/players relationship in relatively successful counties such as Cork (more than once), Waterford, Limerick, Clare, Galway, Offaly and Wexford to name some of the main ones. It is not my assertion that the manager was always wrong in these situations.

In fact, I am certain the manager was far from being the main cause of a couple of these high profile rows.

However, it would appear that in some of the aforementioned instances there were some serious misunderstandings as players and management saw things quite differently, leading to strife and disruption. A lesson from all of these rows is that having a common goal (wanting the team to win) is not sufficient if there are diametrically opposite views on how that goal might be achieved.

Even at club level, it is in your interest to ensure everyone is one hundred percent clear, from the beginning, on how the relationship is supposed to function.

SUMMARY

1. Know what areas will need to be covered.

2. Know who you would like to have on board.

3. Go outside the club, if necessary, for advice and help in putting the management team in place.

4. Listen to the people you have entrusted but remember at a push, you have the final say.

5. Put the best possible structure in place, with a united management team .

6. Seek to present a professional approach which will be respected by the players.

7. Allocate responsibilities to your management team and make sure they clearly understand what is expected of them.

8. The management line-up will vary from sport to sport.

CHAPTER 3
ATTENTION TO DETAIL
Frequently Asked Questions

"The difference between something good and something great is attention to detail." **Charles R.Swindoll, US Christian evangelist**

What should we eat? Can we go to the gym? Can we do weights? Where's the physio? Has anyone got a first aid kit?

There are some miscellaneous issues which will arise, of direct concern to the newly appointed manager. They include players' dietary recommendations, use of a gymnasium, whether or not to use weights as part of a fitness regime and the health related factors such as access to a physiotherapist and basic first-aid. A properly organised management team will have considered such issues and made whatever provisions are deemed necessary.

DIETARY ADVICE

Your trainer may well be in a position to talk about diet to your players. If not, you should find someone suitably qualified to outline the do's and don'ts of eating and drinking for people preparing for serious competitive sport. In this respect, my advice would be to avoid any dramatic regimes.

I heard of a county senior football manager tell senior players whom he had taken away for a training weekend, to have breakfast on Saturday morning consisting of steak and peanuts.

You don't need to be a qualified food scientist or dietician to comment. Just apply a little common sense. How do you go about sourcing someone with dietary knowledge? It is vitally important you have a good relationship with the club chairperson or vice-chair. Then you have a channel through which you can make reasonable requests.

I would say, a good example would be asking does anyone on the committee have a contact with someone who can advise on diet. The chances are high that you will get a contact this way. If not, and if you have to incur cost in getting someone in via a request to your local GP or pharmacist for example, you will have established that as no one within could offer help, you had to go outside.

Having such a person talk to the team after training some night has psychological as well as practical benefits. The players realise you are serious about team preparation and that you are paying attention to details which can give them an edge. If this is done at the beginning of the year and some notes issued to panel members, it becomes a matter of reminding people thereafter. The expert does not need to keep coming back.

There are some facts related to nutrition, knowledge of which will be no burden to the manager.

The principal categories of food are:

Simple carbohydrates:	Fruit, honey, cane sugar
Complex carbohydrates:	Bread, cereals, oats, wheat, rice, pasta, vegetables.
Proteins:	Lean beef, pork, lamb, skinless poultry, fish, eggs, low fat milk, cheese, yoghurt.
Fats:	Butter, margarine, mayonnaise, oil, fatty meat and poultry, full cream cheese, chocolate, fried foods, processed meats.

A recommended diet for someone engaged in a sport such as football, might look like this: 60% carbohydrates: 15% protein: 25% fat.

Those engaged in team sports expend more energy than the average person. Energy may be obtained from all categories of food but carbohydrates are the ideal source.

Carbohydrates are stored in muscle and in the liver as glycogens. Glycogen is the form of energy which is called upon during exercise. Running low on carbohydrates will lead to fatigue.

Proteins give the body its shape and structure.

Fats should be avoided before physical activity as they take longer to digest, but they have a place in a balanced diet.

Note: The aforementioned is basic information intended to give some idea of how foods work in terms of a sports person's dietary requirements.

However, I stress the need to take professional advice from a suitably qualified person before laying down any dietary regulations for the team.

Such advice should go into much greater detail as to which components of each category will be most/least beneficial as well as the timing of food intake in the different categories. The instructions should also include details on what food and especially what fluids should be consumed so as to remain hydrated and especially to aid recovery after strenuous activity.

The GPA (Gaelic Players Association) website contains very good advice on nutrition.

THE GYM

I would issue a word of caution regarding making arrangements for players to use a gymnasium. Frequently, clubs, with the best will in the world, cut a deal with a local gym whereby team members receive membership at discounted rates and very often the club pays part or more likely all of the fees out of scarce resources. It sounds great. "We have got gym membership for the team so our fitness problems are solved."

Outside of team sports, it is a general rule of gym membership that people, all of whom pay their own way, invariably use the facilities less than they had planned. From experience, people whose membership is paid for them, whatever their initial enthusiasm, tend not to avail of the gift.

For every two players who accept the membership and avail of the gym three others will drop out, come up with excuses and waste the club's money. I am not saying "do not take a team to the gym regularly".

What I am saying is "be sure the programme prescribed for them is correct and appropriate – and be sure, before incurring costs, that the programme being put in place will be fully utilised".

WEIGHT PROGRAMMES/ FITNESS REGIMES

Weight programmes may have their place in building strength in players. They also bulk up players and speed and agility may be sacrificed for strength. Also, a weight programme may have to be followed for two or three years to achieve optimum results. Do you have the time and do your players and /or club members have the patience, the commitment, the money?

There has been much talk about upper body strength but it is not much use having a team full of players with fantastic upper body strength if they cannot run quickly, or even more fundamentally, kick or strike a ball with accuracy.

Question every expert and every stated fact, not necessarily loudly but at least in your own mind. Keeping it simple is usually the best way to go, when you have looked at all the possibilities.

It is also worth remembering that in any squad of players there will be a divergence of height, bulk and physical strength. Based on nothing more than the law of averages, it is likely that a handful of your players will benefit from bulking up through a weights programme. Again, you do not need to be an expert. Get a qualified person at the gym to advise on a suitable programme based on your specified needs.

Of course, rugby differs from the other team sports mentioned in that there are quite different requirements for forwards and backs in rugby and this will be reflected in aspects of the respective fitness regimes for the different category of players.

I have worked with a trainer whose background was the Irish army. He introduced medicine balls to outdoor training instead of taking the team to the gym. He reasoned that the gym work would take too long, that we could combine fitness sessions with some ball work and this proved useful. He made the point that the time spent going to and from the gym would be better spent working on basic skills.

It is still an amateur game and getting players to train more than twice a week was problematic. We had 12 medicine balls which worked for up to 24 players – about the maximum we ever had on a senior panel. We trained in the field with the trainer supervising work that included strength exercises with the medicine balls and running, for stamina at first, and later for speed.

At different times we did 30/40 minutes ball work

before or after the physical fitness sessions. At first we did the ball work after the warm-up and finally moved on to the hard physical stuff. Later, as progress was being made, we sometimes left the ball work until after the physical session to see how players functioned when tired and to get them functioning better with the ball even though they were tired.

Note that my comments on the use of a weights programme are related to Gaelic games but different sports will require another approach. For example, in a rugby club team, it would be quite usual to have a fitness and conditioning coach who would put the squad through a weights session every week during the playing season, with the emphasis very much on the requirement for power.

Again, this is specialised. As the manager, you do not need to know how to implement this programme but you need to know it is necessary and where to get a person suitably qualified to oversee it.

MEDICAL CARE/PHYSIOTHERAPY/ FIRST AID

All representative teams have a doctor and physiotherapist on hand during games. Clubs will find it more difficult to have that degree of professionally qualified expertise on tap at all times. Cost will be the main barrier. However, every club should have a relationship with a GP to whom injured players may be referred.

Similarly, in an ideal world, the club should have access to a physiotherapist who attends training sessions and games. In the absence of an ever-present physio, it is possible and it should be mandatory that a designated person, qualified in the basics of first aid, attends all games and training sessions.

This may require you to attend and/or have another member of the management team attend courses which are easily accessible throughout the country.

Costs associated with these courses should be borne by the club. This is one of the issues you will need to address upon your assumption of the managerial role. Whatever the sport, you now have a duty-of-care to the players in your squad.

Prevention of injuries ought to be a consideration for everyone involved in the management of the team. Correct training methods, proper warm-up and warm-down routines are all essential in this respect. In contact sports such as Gaelic football and rugby, technique has to be taught so that unnecessary injuries are avoided.

Over the course of a season, every team suffers some degree of disruption through injury. A consciousness of the need to ensure correct methods are in place to avoid the "stupid" injuries, is a good starting point for the trainer, coach and manager.

Rehabilitation after injury is also important and this is where medical advice from a physiotherapist or sometimes a GP, will be needed.

A point worth noting, regarding injuries, is that keen players will usually want to get back playing as quickly as possible after injury. You will definitely need professional help, usually that of a physiotherapist as from time to time you try to establish if a player has fully recovered. There is history, even at the highest levels, of players apparently passing fitness tests, only to break down in the first game, and quite often, early in that game.

Fitness tests must be carried out rigorously, the player tested thoroughly, so you do not find yourself requiring a replacement much sooner than you had expected while also possibly creating psychological damage to the team.

Much better to acknowledge that the player is not fit and take the time to get the rest of the team focused on covering his/her absence with maximum concentration and effort on their part.

Put simply, it is a setback to lose a key player well ahead of a big game. But you have time to adjust. You are deprived of that time if the said key player persuades you of his/her fitness and then comes a cropper during the game.

With regard to players welfare and well-being, notwithstanding the fact that players will have been advised about hydration, it is an important responsibility of management to have an adequate supply of drinking water and/or isotonic drinks available at all training sessions and games.

SUMMARY

1. Your management team may have the knowledge and answers to these questions on diet, gym, weights and medical issues.

2. If not, make enquiries and make provisions where necessary especially for health/injury related matters.

3. You do not need to be able to answer every question. You need to know where to go for the answers.

4. Don't take chances with issues such as weights programmes and dietary advice. Make sure the correct procedures are followed.

5. Correct training methods can help prevent unnecessary injuries.

6. Fitness tests need to be rigorous and ideally they should be supervised by a physiotherapist.

CHAPTER 4

THE PSYCHOLOGICAL CONTRACT

"When I was a young coach I used to say, treat everybody alike. That's bull. Treat everybody fairly." **Bear Bryant, coach to the University of Alabama, Crimson Tide, football team – the subject of the 1984 film 'The Bear'**

Just as you have got clarity of purpose, an understanding of the responsibilities, and agreement on how they are to be allocated among the management team, it is vital that you get the same clarity of purpose and of understanding with the playing squad. A way of looking at what you are seeking here is to equate it to something called the Psychological Contract, which applies in the business world.

One definition of the Psychological Contract is that it represents the mutual beliefs, perceptions, and informal obligations between an employer and an employee. It sets the dynamic for the relationship and defines the detailed practicality of the work to be done.

While your relationship and that of your management team with the players is not identical to that between employer and employee, it appears to me there are sufficient similarities so that the Psychological Contract is a good place to start.

In more simple English, it can be summarised as the basis of the relationship between the two sides – what they expect from you and what you expect from them. A management team is making commitments and promises to the players, such as:

1. Everything will be in place when you arrive for training.

2. There will be no shortage of equipment.

3. Training sessions will be structured and enjoyable.

4. Over the season, the training programme will evolve so you will be well prepared for competition.

5. Injured players will be provided with the best treatment, within reason.

6. The team will be selected on certain criteria such as attitude and attendance at training.

7. All decisions taken by management will have the good of the team as a priority.

8. The management will establish a game-plan/ method best suited to the players available.

9. Every player will know precisely what is expected from him/her in the particular role within the team.

10. Selected teams will be announced a few days before the championship/important games.

11. Any player being dropped will be told so as well as why, in advance, in a one-to-one meeting with the manager.

The flip side of that Psychological Contract or understanding is that management expects certain things of players such as;

1. They will turn up consistently and punctually for training/coaching sessions.

2. If they ever have a problem in that regard they will notify management through the pre- agreed channel.

3. They will behave like athletes and abstain from wrong diet and alcohol during periods laid down by management, in advance of important games – and agreed at the outset of your tenure.

4. They will always have correct equipment such as boots appropriate to weather conditions (i.e. they will not be seen slipping and sliding on a wet pitch because they insist on wearing blades when a studded boot is needed), laces, studs, correct team shorts if that is their responsibility.

5. They will exercise discipline at all times as long as they are a member of the panel, both on and off the field – always upholding the reputation of the club.

6. They will notify you of any unusual holiday arrangements or plans at the start of the year (I'm thinking weddings here, as an example) so you can have the longest possible notice in order to make a case to the relevant fixture-making body, and to influence dates for key fixtures.

7. They will accept criticism providing it is constructive and dished out in the appropriate manner.

8. They will support each other and management and function like a team rather than a group.

It is not sufficient to note these points, assuming everyone understands them. It is important, at the outset, to explain to the players as a body, that management sees its role as meeting the various requirements as outlined here. The players should know that management believes it has these obligations to the players and that it is the intention to see that players' needs are well served in relation to every one of these points.

It is not sufficient to tell players, "everything will be done to help - we will be great guys, while you will train like maniacs, and then we will win all round us". Outlining the various specific ways in which you will meet your side of the Psychological Contract will demonstrate to the players that you have thought about every aspect of what will be required to bring success. It will show that from the off, you are organised and that they are entering a professionally run set-up.

Equally, spelling out to the players just what is expected of them is critical. You do not want misunderstanding and indeed, everything you are doing here is designed to ensure the ground rules are clear and to avoid misunderstandings.

You also need to give thought to how you will treat breaches of these ground rules. Again, it is in everyone's interest to spell this out at the beginning. A typical example in Gaelic football will be an agreed ban on drinking for, say, a fortnight before a championship game. What will you do if two of your senior players are found in a pub, knocking back pints of stout, just four days before the game?

You would like to think that having taken every step

possible to generate a spirit of co-operation all round, this could not happen. Speaking from experience, anything is possible.

In my case I called the offending players aside at the beginning of training the following night. I asked them was it correct that they were drinking the previous night. They said they were but that other players had broken the rule at other times. I replied that I was unaware of other breaches but that if any were reported to me I would confront the accused as I was now doing with them. They then decided that was the end of the issue and started to walk away at which point I called them back and told them they would not tog out on the following Sunday as they were now off the panel for that one game. Despite everything that had been agreed they responded in shock that such a step would be taken. But they had acknowledged breaking the rules and I had no choice but to take action if I wished to retain any credibility as a manager.

Because I had been aware of a drink culture at the club, I had painstakingly, and probably tediously, gone to each player in turn at the meeting where the drinking ban was agreed. Each player was asked "do you agree to stay off drink for this period until the championship game is played?" Each player had to answer for himself.

On reflection, I was glad I had taken that step because had I made it a general question, moving on when there were no negative answers, I know I might have had more difficulty in dealing with my two drinkers. I could well have got a response that they either had never agreed or that one (or both) of them was absent/ at the toilet/out of the room, when this had been discussed.

One point well worth bearing in mind is that while you can spell out rules and warn that sanctions will be taken against people who break those rules, it is not advisable to list the punishment for each offence. Leave yourself some slack. Do not back yourself into a corner where you have no option but to impose a pre-determined punishment.

In many of the well-publicised cases where the manager/player relationship became dysfunctional, it would appear there was no understanding of the Psychological Contract. If there had been, the difficulties and misunderstandings might not have occurred or might have been identified and addressed in the correct spirit at a much earlier stage.

Put simply, if it is spelt out and agreed at the outset what we will do for you and what we, in turn, expect of you, it is more difficult for someone to shirk responsibility for a problem later in the relationship. Much of this may seem like common sense. The problem is that common sense is not always that common.

I cannot overstate how important I regard this particular issue. The rows between managers and playing groups appear to spring from misunderstandings and allegedly broken promises. They spring from perceived sleights and contrasting interpretations of what each side thought was clearly understood – or which one side later choose to think was clearly stated or understood. Poor communication skills, people thinking they have made something clear, when they have actually made an ambiguous statement, people hearing what they want to hear and later claiming the bit they ignored was never actually said, all contribute to the breakdowns, most or all of which were avoidable.

A topical and perhaps not so untypical example of a dysfunctional management/team relationship appears in Tony Griffin's account of the set-up in Clare hurling in 2009. (*Screaming At The Sky – My Journey,* by Tony Griffin).

"At the heart of a professional set-up is a basic respect for the people you work with. As a player, you sense this in the way you are spoken to and dealt with, and this becomes more important than expensive gear or the right jerseys. It's more important than running a training session on time or laying out an itinerary for your players. Sometimes the voice of the management felt like a lead balloon. You can take one night of being shouted at. You can actually take three or four. But after weeks and months the air remains septic even though the words have lost their bite. The negatives were accentuated and without a win, or anything positive to cling to, those negatives grew out of all proportion. "How the f*** do ye expect to win playing like that?" This was one of the central themes of the year."

These last quoted comments strike me as the polar opposite to the honesty and respect for individuals that are common traits among many of the most successful managers.

SUMMARY

1. Spell out to the players what you see as your responsibility and that of your management team.

2. Spell out what is expected of the players.

3. Get agreement at the start as to the standards that will apply.

4. Deal with problems firmly but quietly.

5. Treat people with respect at all times, even when taking disciplinary action.

CHAPTER 5

GROUP OR TEAM

"Individual commitment to a group effort- that is what makes a team work" **Vince Lombardi, American football coach**

"It is not accidental that sporting teams range from around seven or eight to 15-a-side. For a true group cannot exist with much less than seven members; and with more than 20 it tends to become a crowd. Two is not a group; they may combine well together, but too much hangs on the individuals and how well they get on. Threes tend to divide into a two and a one; fours into two-two. Five or six people can make a group, but the absence of one or two individuals makes its identity precarious. Sports teams are, then, big enough for the group to have a character of its own, and for there to be significant division of roles.

"They are small enough for communication to be simple, for individuality to be maintained, and for each player to know the others extremely well, at least in the setting of sport. Such groups are the descendants of primitive hunting bands. The well-being of large companies also depends on the functioning of these small teams within them, from the girls behind the counter to the board of directors."

Mike Brearley – 'The Art of Captaincy'

Have you inherited a group or a team? What is the difference between a group and a team?

Within a group, the individual may function as an individual, without concern or care for the group as a whole. The individual will typically be focused on his/her own objectives. For example, in a work situation, he/she will set personal goals in conjunction with the manager and will have his/her own responsibilities clearly defined.

By contrast, in a team structure, the person will be focused on the team objectives, to which their own individual goals must take a secondary place. The responsibilities will be defined by the manager but this will be done in conjunction with the team members.

Where the structure is a team, every member or component will put the team ahead of themselves. They will truly be team players rather than solo artists. This is one of the challenges facing any new manager of a sports team. How do you deal with the player who truly believes they are more important than the team, that without them, not only would the team fail, but the club itself would probably disintegrate?

Most managers including some of the very successful ones, tend to try to get the maverick to fit into the team. Any objective study would show mixed or patchy results. Most examples are in professional games where replacements can be bought or traded. There have been examples in county teams such as Mayo and Dublin where the "different" player eventually bowed out or was left out.

An interesting take on the subject is outlined in the Michael M Lewis book, *Moneyball – The Art of Winning an Unfair Game*. It tells the story of the Oakland Athletics baseball team and its manager, Billy Beane. The team, operating on a budget which is a fraction of that enjoyed by its competitors, consistently qualifies for play-offs and exceeds expectations. One of the guiding principles of Beane is that he will not touch any player with a history of insubordination or poor discipline of any kind.

His rationale is that it's a team game. No manager or coach should have to spend inordinate time worrying about or having to deal with the unorthodox behaviour of one player, no matter how talented. It is simply not good for forging a team spirit and ethic, he believes. Billy Beane will sign a talented player who is overweight or lacking in strength – because these deficiencies can be sorted out. He will not sign the most talented player in America if that player is in the words of my favourite referee – "a bollix" – see section on discipline.

As a leader you will have to drive towards having a team ethic, an attitude born from hard work and the knowledge that improvement is achievable in a team context. Mickey Harte has an interesting take on the differences between individuals or as he puts it "respecting uniqueness".

Essentially he appears to be saying you should look at what a player brings to the team, try to tap into how that can help the team while helping the player improve other aspects of his game. His philosophy, as I understand it, is getting what would be seen as the skilful players to work harder on the field while getting the workhorses to chip in with a few vital points when needed.

He also keeps players' morale up by reminding them of what they are good at when they may be discouraged at apparent deficiencies in their own game. This philosophy is very much in line with the John Wooden approach of ensuring that players do not let what they cannot do interfere with what they can do.

As a manager and leader you will put faith in players. Some will deliver and some will let you down. How you react in both instances will have a bearing on success in building a winning team. Remember, if you have set out your approach at the beginning it is easier to enforce rules later. If there are breaches of discipline, they must be addressed.

You may chose to let a first offence slide. Be careful not to be exploited. Any discipline- related dealings between management and a player should be just that – between management and the player and not a topic involving everyone. Be fair and be seen to be fair and you are more likely to be respected.

A thought worth bearing in mind, as we talk about the importance of team over individual is that of former US president Harry Truman. "It's amazing what you can accomplish if you do not care who gets the credit". It is what has made the phenomenally successful and completely humble basketball coach, John Wooden, an icon for so many modern managers.

SOCIAL ASPECTS

Another aspect of whether the body of people whom

you are managing consists of group or real team is the extent to which they bond. Without a doubt, it is an advantage to have a united group, with a singular attitude, or at least as near to a singular approach as is possible. The unity of the team will definitely be enhanced if they tend to socialise as a group.

There is the famous quote about Nemo Rangers players that you never see one on his own. In his autobiography "Rebel, Rebel", Billy Morgan attributes that comment to Frank Cogan. Billy and Frank are two men who epitomise the spirit of Nemo, having been lifelong members of what is the most successful football club in Ireland, and having shared in those remarkable triumphs at county, provincial and national level. Clearly they both take pride in the fact that Nemo lads tend to be friends off the field as much as teammates on the field.

The other side of socialising all the time is that it can become just that... socialising all the time. There is a drink culture within certain sports and Gaelic football and hurling offer many examples of teams which drink together and whose drinking exploits far exceed any on-field achievements.

Indeed Billy Morgan refers to the Cork football team during his time as manager, and deals with the problems which arose because on occasions he would join the players for a few drinks, when they were on overnight trips. Billy clearly believed there was a time to relax and to enjoy each other's company. The difficulties this created with a county board, not all of whom would have shared his views, were many. Also, he was referring to a time in the 1980s and 90s.

As time has gone by, there is a perceptible change in how managers view alcohol consumption. The approach to training has become more scientific. Players, or a great many inter-county players at least, have become fastidious about their diet and their general preparation. Bonding and drinking sessions are less popular. Stories of teams winning major competitions immediately after certain team members had a feed of drink, have become a thing of the past.

Tales of the great Brian Clough buying champagne for his full squad of players, the night before a major final, refer to a different age. Clough believed it relaxed his players and enabled them to sleep well. Maybe he was right but it is 30 years ago and it is hard to imagine any of today's successful managers taking this approach.

Drinking is a frequent theme in stories of the GAA Christy O'Connor has written a marvellous book, *The Club*, about a season in the life of his club, St Joseph's Doora-Barefield. It is a study of a year in the club, 10 years on from when they won the All Ireland club title. While there is hardly a line in the book that will not resonate with club members everywhere, the issue of drinking by players and the response of club management is well covered and will strike a familiar chord with anyone who has been involved at club level, in virtually any club in Ireland.

I have heard many stories from other managers (which

matched my own experiences) about how difficult it can be to break that culture, especially, it seems, in country or rural places, although not all town teams escape the curse.

The question, then, is how does one deal with fostering team spirit while not encouraging a drinking culture.

First, here is a story. A friend of mine was managing a football team consisting entirely of young men. The lads started the season well. They trained hard; they won their first few games, before a lull in the fixtures gave them a short break from competition. My friend decided this offered a great opportunity for bonding. So he decided they should have a few beers together.

He bought the beer, arranged a venue (not a pub) and insisted they all attend and partake in the bonding exercise. He himself would not be there. This was to be a team building event where the lads got to know each other a bit better in a relaxed atmosphere, uninhibited by any management presence. Attendance was not optional. It was mandatory. No excuses would be countenanced as my friend, the manager, considered this every bit as important as a training session or even a game.

In the event, all of the squad turned up – with one exception. One player decided he had a greater need to bond with his new girlfriend than with his new team mates. Next day the manager heard that all had gone well but that there had been the one absentee. So he called the culprit and read the riot act. He finished by telling the poor lad that he would meet him at the beginning of the next training session and inform him whether he was still a part of the panel or not. In reality, he did not intend taking any action against the poor love-struck young fellow. After all, as he said to me when relating the story, "we have all had problems throwing lads off panels for drinking, but this could well have been a first, throwing a guy out for not drinking".

Now, to answer the earlier question of what to do, it should be borne in mind that there are more ways to go out together and bond, without necessarily spending the entire time drinking. There are even ways to vary routines which help the team-building process and which do not involve drink in any shape or form.

The simplest example is a change to the training routine. Change location. Go somewhere else. Do something completely different. Constantly working in the same place, in the same way, can become tedious. I recall in Castletown, the trainer taking the team on a run down to the nearby beach where they removed their footwear and ran in the ocean parallel with the shore. Work was done, the players bitched about the freezing cold water, but they remembered it long after other regular sessions were forgotten.

In Christy O'Connor's *The Club*, he describes something very similar as his hurling team, St Joseph's Doora-Barefield, journeyed out to do a training session on the beach near the home of Kilmurray Ibrickane, the well-known football club from west Clare. As Christy puts it, no one remembered to check the times of the tides so when they got there the tide was fully in. He describes how they then played hurling on the Kilmurray back pitch before heading across the road to the Atlantic, or the biggest ice bath around. The point though is that the trip was a variation from the usual routine and would be remembered with affection by the players, no matter how much they complained at the time about the cold of the sea.

I have heard of teams going to paintball centres where mock warfare takes place with paint pellets instead of live ammunition. Various types of camps are utilised by teams, where, for example, a military type of training involving abseiling, scaling walls or high netting, climbing through tubes or over hurdles makes for an interesting diversion and an opportunity for team building. It is about the shared experience that you can collectively look back on later on.

It is worth planning some such diversions. Get a committee of the players themselves to work with you in coming up with researched suggestions. Maybe visit a rifle-range on a Saturday morning followed by some different activity and a meal together. There are various activity centres around the country where these exercises may be carried out without great cost to anyone. Many greyhound stadia have been upgraded and offer attractive packages to groups. Sponsored racedays or golf outings may cost a bit more but they could still offer potential opportunities to bring the team together away from the usual routine.

I do not wish to appear to be going down the politically correct, health and safety, route but just one word of warning might be appropriate. Always keep in mind that as manager you have a duty of care to the members of your playing panel.

In recent years, a then Premier League football team in England, took a group of young players to a military training centre, where they were to spend some time training like soldiers under the supervision of military trainers. The exercise went horribly wrong when a young footballer got into difficulties while the group, as part of one exercise, was wading across a river. The lad drowned and very nearly pulled another two lads down with him. It does no harm to keep in mind the need to ensure that whatever is being done is subject to a safety regime that does not place anyone in danger.

We come back then to the more orthodox bonding exercises. Some teams or clubs will have an annual weekend away. A good time to have this is early in the season, after the initial training programme has got underway, but well before serious championship stuff has commenced.

Maybe the trip can involve a challenge/friendly game. Establishing contacts with clubs in various distant locations is not difficult. In February and March, hotels are none too busy and deals can be had. A bit of sightseeing or a round of golf is possible virtually anywhere in Ireland. Be aware that an away trip whether it includes a challenge game or not will be a drinking and "letting off steam" exercise. That's part of the GAA It is a part of the culture. There's a time and a place for everything so do not go on such a trip with any intention of cramping people's style or with the notion that the challenge game will be taken seriously.

Based on some experiences I've had (though not while manager) you will be doing well to get 15 bodies onto a field the day after the night before. Be prepared but be prepared to relax too. There will be time enough for banning drink and trying to enforce that when it really matters. Regarding this weekend away, set a deadline by which time it must have taken place. Don't leave the possibility that it becomes delayed and then occurs at a time when perhaps league points are important and you find your team returning on a Monday from a "great" weekend away, and going into what has become a vital league game on the Tuesday night. It has been known to happen.

You may be fortunate to find the players, to a man, (or woman) are friends off the field. Maybe they have that Nemo Rangers culture of always being seen in each other's company. It is more likely that some effort is required to foster a spirit of togetherness. Simple efforts can help, such as arranging to have tea and sandwiches at team meetings and creating an informal atmosphere before and after the meetings.

It may not be feasible to provide food after all training sessions but this could be done perhaps on a specific occasion such as early in the week of a big game. The point is that the smallest efforts can help and the difference between winning and losing can come down to the small details. That additional bit of togetherness and spirit might just be the inches that make a difference.

SUMMARY

1. Stress the importance of team over individual.

2. Always base your own judgements on what is best for the team.

3. Don't let players become negative about what they cannot do.

4. Deal with issues fairly

5. Deal with problems firmly but as quietly and privately as possible.

6. Encourage social involvement among team members.

7. If there is no great bond, organise events to help foster one.

8. Insist that all players participate – drawing the line by not banning someone who fails to join the drinking session!

CHAPTER 6
CREATING CHANGE

"Be not the first by whom the new one tried,
Nor yet the last to lay the old aside."
Alexander Pope, Essay On Criticism

The poet has a point. Because something is new and trendy is no reason to dive in – most people would be slow to spend their money on new untried technology. Equally, dismissing something simply because it has been around a long time does not make sense.

While most of the literature on "change" and "management of change" deals with how to implement change, I would advise you to do a mental audit before you plunge into making changes. Is change necessary? Does it need to be drastic or radical? What needs to be changed? Ask yourself these questions before commencing the process.

However, it is indeed a rare situation in which a manager is appointed with the brief to keep things the same. Usually the task is to bring about change – and that desired change usually amounts to improving matters. This is as true of business as it is of sport.

The leading expert on the subject of change in the business world is Dr John P Kotter of Harvard Business School. He has devised an eight-step programme towards bringing about change in an organisation. My point in referring to it is that whether you are managing a team from a small club or indeed a large business, while there is significantly more at stake in the latter, and for a larger body of people, both are organisations and the fundamental issues still need to be addressed if change is successfully to be achieved.

Also, while the schedule as set out by Dr Kotter may seem extravagant in terms of your club, take a look at what he considers the key steps and see what makes sense or what is applicable in your set of circumstances.

1. Establish a sense of urgency.
2. Form a guiding coalition.
3. Create a vision.
4. Communicate the vision.
5. Empower the people to act on the vision.
6. Create quick wins.
7. Consolidate improvements.
8. Institutionalise the new approaches – change the culture.

The first point is clear and needs no qualification – you need all concerned to understand that there are limitations on how long changes can take, that people need to address problems with a degree of urgency, that improvements must be introduced sooner rather than later, if success is to be achieved.

The guiding coalition is your management team and the vision is what you agree it to be – the overarching objective – the goals. Having decided upon your goals, clearly you will want every team member on board so from there on it will be about ensuring they have a clear understanding of those goals but also that you and your management team produce an easily understood plan on how you propose to reach those goals. I believe this is one of the most important elements in terms of team management.

It is all very well to say – "this is our goal – this is what we have all agreed we intend achieving" but the management's job is to outline HOW you all intend achieving the agreed objective – achieving your dream. From a team management perspective, quick wins in this context may well be quick wins in games, but the more deep meaning is correcting some of the obviously wrong aspects of the set-up into which you have gone – correcting the wrongs that are easiest to correct. It will almost always be true that the bigger problems take a bit longer to solve.

When you have made small but important changes for the better (quick wins) you then need to ensure those changes are maintained and that the previous way is banished for good. Changing the culture is something you do, or rather something that results from all the other beneficial changes you have made. So do not get hung up on it as an objective in itself. Make the changes that need to be made.

As you and your coalition bring about improvement, the culture will also improve. As you get to know your playing personnel you will soon see what needs changing and what may be left alone. Change for its own sake does not make much sense and given the limitations of time, people are better served if your time is spent taking actions and making changes that produce a dividend such as improved team spirit.

One last point about change is that you will encounter different responses to your efforts to bring about change, particularly if what you are attempting is in any way radical. Therefore, I cannot stress how important it is to get your own management team fully committed and then to get the players equally committed. The leaders among the players will be vital in this respect. If the senior members of the team are supportive, your chances of success are magnified.

There is always cynicism, and a dressing room is feeding ground for such a response. You may be assured that radical change will be viewed with suspicion by some club members not directly involved. It is then essential that your players are not diverted and unduly influenced by this type of reaction. By having the leaders on board from the beginning you save yourself much hardship later.

Keep in mind that whether in business or sport, those who have achieved great things have invariably done so through changing the organisation or the culture. John Wooden had an interesting take on change, offering the opinion that failure is not fatal but failure to change might be.

SUMMARY

1. Make sure the change is necessary.

2. Make sure the planned change is appropriate.

3. Get buy-in from your management team.

4. Get buy-in from the players.

5. Create a sense of urgency.

6. Go for the quick wins to get momentum.

CHAPTER 7

COMMUNICATION

"The problem with communication is the illusion that it has occurred." **George Bernard Shaw**

Communication is a vitally important part of management in any walk of life, no less so in your role as manager of your club team. Firstly, a definition: communication may be defined as the process by which information is exchanged and understood by two or more people, usually with the intent to motivate or influence behaviour.

A Harvard professor once asked a class to define communication by drawing a picture. Most of the class drew someone writing or speaking with a speech bubble beside their mouth. He dismissed all such drawings saying they had failed to capture the essence of communication as its true meaning is "to share" rather than "to speak" or "to write." The distinction between sharing and proclaiming is one that any manager would do well to remember.

It is estimated that managers in business spend 80 per cent of their time communicating. That is 48 minutes in every hour, in meetings, talking informally, on the telephone or emailing. A manager of a club team may not spend quite as high a percentage of his/her time communicating, but it is an enormous part of the job.

If one considers the time such a manager spends, especially on the telephone, speaking with members of the management or playing team and pursuing team business, it becomes clear that communication is going on continuously and not just when all are together for training, practice, or a game.

If there is good communication at all the various levels, life will be considerably easier and management is likely to be that much more enjoyable. At the beginning of this book I referred to your role and how it interfaces with club management, i.e. The club executive in the form of the chairperson and secretary and probably the treasurer as well. If, through good communication, you have established your responsibilities and entitlements then there should be minimal problems later on.

1. Are you entitled to spend money on equipment, renting meeting rooms, renting pitches, transport, laundry etc? Was there a clear agreement at the start on all of these matters and was there a procedure put in place so that when something unforeseen cropped up there was a pre-agreed point of contact so that you got quick answers to your query? No club chairperson or treasurer likes to see unexpected bills arrive from bus companies, physiotherapists etc.

Therefore, it should be agreed in advance, where possible, what categories of expenditure can be incurred and what can be spent without clearance and what exceptional items might need clearance from the executive. If there is good communication between the team manager and his management team with the designated person on the club executive, things will run more smoothly.

2. Communication with the relevant administrative body for your sport, at least with its fixtures secretary is also important. Once again, look at that person's priorities – to get games played with the minimum number of postponements or cancellations.

Someone on your management team should be the designated contact. Most people are reasonable if they are treated reasonably. Set your priorities for the year. You will, in all likelihood need the fixture secretary's co-operation at some point, maybe in relation to an important championship fixture.

Use your common sense. Do not seek changes unless necessary. If you know of a problem well in advance, make contact as early as possible notifying them, in writing if necessary. Put yourself in their position. I have seen fixtures secretaries respond quite differently to people who were consistently unhelpful and to people who tried to be co-operative. Needless to say, the response reflected the way they had been treated. As with all officialdom, they are only human, even if it doesn't seem so at times!

3. Communication with the players is much easier in the 21st century than in times gone by. I recall a time when players were notified of games by postcard. It seems hard to believe now, but putting a communication system in place is easier than ever. Mobile phone texts are the most efficient way of communicating with a large number of people.

Any network provider will set up a system whereby texts may be sent through a computer. The sender types in the message and sends it to a pre-ordained grouping.

There may be restrictions on the number of characters permitted per group message, but this system is adequate and cost-effective as well as time effective, for mass communication with the playing panel.

Emails make it easier than ever to keep in contact with and provide information to a large group of people. In keeping with other ground rules, all members must provide their mobile phone number and email address and must notify management should these change. If the contact point for players is a member of your back-up team other than yourself, clearly you will need to be kept informed of any queries from players or non-standard responses to the group messages.

While you may have appointed one of your number as secretary to the management team and the contact point for players, you should also have all players mobile numbers yourself. And the players should have the numbers of the various management members, something which is easily supplied on a small printed card.

4. Make sure you and your contact person have contact numbers for others with whom you may have dealings, such as a groundsman (where applicable), doctor, physiotherapist, masseur, and any club officials with whom you are likely to have dealings.

COMMUNICATION BETWEEN MANAGER AND PLAYER

The more fundamental aspect of communication between the manager and the players is the very foundation of the relationship. This cannot be dealt with by reference to mobile phones and will ultimately decide how successful you all become.

Will you behave like an autocratic leader – my way or the highway? Will you lay out the rules, allowing no flexibility whatsoever? Will you outline the rules and allow the most trying members of your playing panel to lead you a merry dance? In other words, how will you communicate with your players and how will they communicate with you?

A fundamental, difficult and challenging aspect of your communication with your players is the variation in backgrounds between players. There will inevitably be a wide range of educational backgrounds: of social backgrounds and even of literacy, in a typical club team. Your task is to be able to get your message across to this cross section of society – this society in microcosm that you will refer to as your team. There will be players who "get it" first time and others who will take a lot of patience, cajoling or maybe browbeating, to get an understanding of what it is you are communicating to the team.

The first point I would make to any inexperienced team manager is – "you are in charge". That will be clear to the players from the start, so it should not be necessary to remind people of the fact.

For instance, you will not need to say "I'm the boss – I'm the gaffer", to quote one example.

Your communication with the players will come by way

of meetings where everyone must be given an opportunity to raise any relevant points and in one-to-one chats which should also be an important part of your work with the team. Meetings should have a specific purpose and while written agendas are not necessary for a team meeting, you should make it clear why you are getting together.

Typically, team meetings will be to discuss a forthcoming game, to announce the team and agree the game plan or you may meet to review a game you have played. A common way to arrange pre-game meetings is after the final training session prior to a game. If you are playing a championship game on Sunday, you will probably train on Friday night and meet afterwards to announce the team and discuss your plans.

When the team is to be announced, it is very unlikely you will have problems with players being unavailable for a meeting which will run a little later than a normal training session. If it is after a training session, wherever the venue, try to arrange tea and sandwiches to bring some degree of warmth and informality to the proceedings, as well as creating the environment for better communication.

For a review meeting, it is a good idea to hold it in the changing room before the first training session after a game, i.e. probably on a Tuesday night after a weekend game. Set a time limit but ask players to contribute. Do not be afraid to ask players to analyse their own game. Do not be afraid to refer to the management team.

If your communication is to be open and geared to

engender mutual trust you should be prepared to analyse your performance and to declare for example, that you should have made a positional switch or substitution earlier or in a different way. People will respect honesty. Don't be too self critical, undermining confidence in management but if there is a problem, recognise it, declare it and vow to not have it recur.

One-to-one conversations are particularly useful when dealing with players. They can be carried out at training or during a coaching session, provided you are not the trainer or coach. You need to know how a player feels about his/her own form. You want to assess how confident he/she is. You may need to reassure some players and to clarify what you expect of others. You need to know each player understands what is expected of him in his role on the field.

Your ultimate objective is that every player goes out fully confident in their ability to perform a role which they completely understand. Only by talking to them and allowing them to talk will you achieve this. It does not require a lot of talking either. In a couple of minutes with a player you can quickly establish that you are both happy that there is clarity as to what the player must do, come the next game.

And sometimes it may take more than a couple of minutes. Interestingly, Jack O'Connor describes in his autobiography, *Keys of the Kingdom*, several occasions where he went to great lengths to spend some time with a player. Motivated by the need to understand why a particular player was not going as well as usual or how a player was responding to adversity or to a matter unrelated to football, O'Connor took the time and trouble to have a round of golf, a meal or maybe just a cup of coffee with such a player. That is inter-county management, and we are dealing with the more mundane issue of club management here.

However, learn from the best. See how the most successful managers function. In a club situation, you probably have the advantage that most players are geographically closer together and to your own base. So if an issue needs to be dealt with, consider whether it is better done away from the training ground, away from the time constraints that apply before or after training, when someone is under pressure to get away, or someone else wants you out of the dressing rooms so he can lock up.

SUMMARY

1. Communication means sharing not telling.

2. Communication is critical to your success or failure as a manager.

3. You must communicate at several different levels.

4. Communication between you and your players must be as near to perfect as possible.

5. You must be certain your message is understood and, critically, you must listen and heed the communication to you from your management team and from your players.

CHAPTER 8
STRATEGY

"Hope is not a strategy." **Warren Buffett, Chairman and CEO Berkshire Hathaway (the Sage of Omaha)**

Strategy is generally understood, in this context, to mean how your team will be set up or how they will play. If your coach is a separate person and you are not fulfilling both roles of coach and manager, then the coach may have some thoughts on how the team should play. As manager, it is your call. Besides, your own coaching experience should come into play when devising the best strategy or method for your team.

The best advice I can offer is to follow the KISS principle – Keep It Simple, Stupid. Don't get hung up on systems which may confuse rather than inspire the players. Ultimately your system or method will depend on the players at your disposal. Assess what you have available to you and play as simple a system as possible, making sure your management colleagues and players fully understand and are comfortable with whatever the strategy may be. One piece of advice I would offer is that you have a fall-back plan in case the main system is not working. Again, it is vital that the players understand this.

Even a successful system will, one day, run into a brick wall. It is better for all concerned that there is a clearly understood alternative and that this fall-back has been practised with just such an eventuality in mind. Put simply: have a Plan B.

Soccer probably offers the best example of how team formations vary over time. As long ago as 1966 when England won the World Cup, Alf Ramsey's 4:3:3 formation was regarded as revolutionary. Since then, 4:4:2 has been the most popular and successful system. Interestingly, an analysis of the systems deployed by the 20 teams in Italy's top division, Serie A, for the 2010-2011 season shows eight different formations were utilised. Four clubs used the 4:4:2 system while four more used 4:3:1:2.

Inter Milan who won the previous five championships as well as a Champions League, deployed a 4:2:3:1 system with Fiorentina the only other team using this formation. A fascinating insight is the comment by Jose Mourinho about Inter's formation under his management. "We were losing to Sienna at home, we switched to three defenders, we won. With these three points we won the championship."

The moral of the story is that there is no 'right' or 'best' system and perhaps a manager has to be prepared to change things around, even in the course of a single game, in order to regain control or change the outcome. While soccer provides the ideal example of varying systems, this applies across all sports.

Rugby teams have to decide whether they will run the ball or kick for possession. The captain in a rugby team has quite a lot of influence in carrying out management instructions. Frequently, it is his call as to whether the team will go through the phases attempting to retain possession or force the opposition into a rash move wherein they may concede a penalty. His alternative could be to instruct a kick for touch, to relieve pressure or gain yardage.

It is fair to say the resources will, or at least should, dictate the strategy. The simplest example is a rugby team which has a massive and powerful pack which can easily overpower any opponents. This team will hardly specialise in running the ball. In any team game, the new manager would do well to assess his assets, the strengths and weaknesses. Then, rather than trying to force the team to play a particular system, ask what suits the players in the squad. Play to the squad's strengths and work on the weaknesses – work on improving those weaknesses and doing everything possible to hide them from the opposition.

INWARD OR OUTWARD

One aspect of managerial style that has often been debated is whether you should be inward looking – focused exclusively on your own team or the opposite – focused heavily on the opposition. I have encountered managers who took the view – "never mind the opposition – let them worry about us".

The most famous example of a manager obsessed with the opposition was the late Don Revie who managed Leeds United and later, England. He was renowned for his dossiers which were distributed to his players and gave detailed assessments of all opposing players. Indeed when Leeds dominated English football they won very few trophies relative to their apparent superiority. Revie's critics maintained he was so taken up with opposition players that he actually undermined his own players' confidence when the vital title clinching games came round. Like most aspects of managing, a degree of balance is necessary.

In Gaelic football and hurling, at club level, most teams have their one or two key players. I firmly believe it would be foolish not to give consideration as to how best to cope with them. It is not necessary to become obsessed but it can surely only inspire confidence in your players if you are seen to have your homework done and to have a plan which increases the chances of winning by reducing the opposition threats. Remember, those threats may not be in the shape of a specific player. There may be something about the way the opposition plays that will pose a problem or perhaps an opportunity for you.

I am reminded of an occasion when I was managing Castletown in a Wexford senior football semi-final. As luck would have it, we were up against Kilanerin in that game. There was only one problem: Mattie Forde. Forde was at his peak around that time and was an absolutely brilliant footballer, capable of winning a game on his own, something he had done time and again.

Now I have two memories of the build-up to that game. The first is simply a good story. Our captain and goalkeeper, Anthony Masterson, was actually sharing a house in Gorey with two other lads, one of whom was the great Mattie. Anthony was being interviewed for local radio and the interviewer, in a long preamble, was outlining the history of rivalry and even hostility in long bygone days between the neighbouring clubs.

The interviewer made reference to relationships having become more amicable in modern times, even to the extent that there had been marriages involving couples from the respective parishes. Anthony, being unused to doing interviews, and perhaps distracted by noise around him, misheard the reference to marriages and just got the bit about relationships having become more friendly. His immediate reply to the inter-marriage comment was "ah yea, sure there are no problems at all, sure Mattie and myself are living together".

A number of Castletown players nearly choked laughing. Poor Anthony was struggling for a while to explain that what he said and what he meant were not quite in synch. I never heard how Mattie responded but I have no doubt he saw the humour in Anthony's embarrassment.

The second (and more relevant) thing I recall in the run-up to that game was our plans to cope with Forde. I had spoken to a few people whose judgement I trusted. The other selectors and I had decided who would man-mark him. We then reckoned we would play a spare man directly in front of him to minimise the amount of ball he could get.

The final person whose views I wished to canvass had himself been a selector with Wexford, so he had ample first-hand knowledge of just how lethal Mattie could be. I put it to him that I was thinking of playing with only five forwards, as the sixth one would be deployed in front of Mattie Forde, and asked him what he thought. He replied, "you could play with two forwards if you could be sure the rest of them could stop Mattie scoring – he's that good."

The point here is that at club level, where you are confronted with an exceptional player or two, it would undoubtedly be wrong to ignore the very real threat. By all means, ensure you have your own house in order but ignore such a player at your peril. The postscript to that story was that the plan worked but Mattie would win another championship before Castletown would.

In 2009 Cork's football team, packed with very tall men around the centre of the field posed a problem for most teams when trying to deal with kick outs. Before the All Ireland semi-final, Tyrone observed that Cork's centre forward, Pearse O'Neill, rather than their midfielders, was the target for their kick-outs. As the Tyrone centre back had a huge height disadvantage, he switched with his own much taller corner back just for Cork kick-outs.

Kerry manager Jack O'Connor reasoned before an All Ireland final that as Mayo had small forwards, their training games mainly would have had low ball delivered to those small men. As a consequence the Mayo backs, he reasoned, would not have been subjected to much high ball during preparation for the All Ireland Final. Kerry elected to bomb high ball in from the word go. The effect was devastating and an All Ireland Final has seldom been over so early.

I have referred to John Wooden on a few occasions in this book. He was phenomenally successful as head coach to the UCLA basketball team, creating a successful dynasty where there had never been success. Wooden passed away in June 2010 a mere four months short of his 100th birthday. In the 12 seasons between 1964 and 1975 under his guidance UCLA won 10 national championships, including seven in a row. This period included a run of 88 consecutive wins. In terms of approach, his philosophy was quite alien to anything else we are likely to encounter.

It may be argued that basketball, as a game, has significant differences from the field games discussed in this book. After all, there are only five players on court at any one time and games are played in an indoor arena. I was prompted to take a harder look at Wooden's philosophies because of the frequency with which his name came up as a figure of influence for so many leaders across a variety of sports. Notwithstanding the differences between sports the results were intriguing. At one level his approach appeared to embrace common sense and many of the same principles or characteristics which recur in the stories of most of the great managers and indeed players.

Wooden believed: "Combined, Industriousness and Enthusiasm create an irreplaceable component of great leadership. Hard work and enthusiasm are contagious. A leader who exhibits them will find the organisation does too."

There it is again. It seems there is no getting away from this hard work, if you want to do well in management. While these sentiments and many more seemed logical and his thinking was full of sound homespun advice, it soon became clear there was so much more to this man. In the context of looking inward or outward, he never spoke about opponents. But then he never spoke about winning a game or a competition.

For those of us who have grown up in a culture of discussing the opposition, discussing objectives always in the context of which competitions we hoped to win, this revelation was truly startling. John Wooden's approach was to seek to get every player to reach his potential, to be the best he could be; and to do that consistently. Then the team, for it was always about the team with John Wooden, had to strive to be the best it possibly could – letting the results take care of themselves.

Concentration on the process, not the outcome, was how it was described. The most successful and best known player to have played for UCLA in those years was Lewis Alcindor, much better known by the name he took when he converted to Islam, Kareem Abdul-Jabbar. This is what he had to say about Wooden's approach: "Winning was never mentioned by him. For coach Wooden it was, 'Fellas, we've got to play our best. Let's do that.' That's a lot different from saying, 'Fellas, we've got to win.' A lot different."

Another member of one of those championship-winning teams, had this to say: "He'd keep telling us, 'Focus on what I'm teaching. Don't focus on the score. Just do what you're supposed to do and things will work out fine. Just play as a team and we'll be fine.' He was always supportive, even when he was correcting something wrong. Most of all he taught us unity and oneness of purpose in what we were doing, namely, working to be the very best we could be – to perform our best out there on the court."

This approach is so radically different to what we would regard as the normal attitude we have encountered as players and that we have adopted as coaches and managers. I believe it offers serious potential if applied with intelligence.

One point I would make is that most of the people I have come across who revere John Wooden, are involved in team games with far more than five people on the team at any one time. In all cases, they were aware of their opposition and I believe, in all cases, they would have included in their strategy, an approach to dealing with key players on opposing teams.

References to people concentrating on the process and letting the outcome take care of itself are rare, especially in sport. Mike Brearley refers to a time when Middlesex had taken off to a sensational start to the season before things suddenly went wrong. He, as captain, and those around him were struggling badly to grasp what had changed, when his teammate, Roland Butcher concluded that they had lost focus as a team by becoming too obsessed with outcomes, already counting trophies, while failing to concentrate on the process.

Brearley understood and brought about the change. Perhaps Roland Butcher was an early follower of John Wooden. I relate the story here because it is a practical example of how the approach worked in a sport which could hardly be more different from basketball.

Most people reading this will be about as familiar as myself with the UCLA basketball programme and its history. Slightly nearer to home, well in Europe at least, is FC Barcelona, a team which most sports fans will have seen regularly, over recent years. By any standards this has to be the most brilliantly attractive football team that any of us has enjoyed watching. I was struck by the words of Pep Guardiola, the Barcelona coach, during an interview after his team had demolished the Mourinho-managed Real Madrid 5–0.

He stressed that what was important was that they had played very well. He went on to point out that the result was simply the outcome, while playing at their high standard was their constant objective. Once again, we have a highly successful modern manager talking about the performance rather than the outcome.

If people as diverse as Wooden and Guardiola thought and think like that, there is a lesson for the rest of us mortals. Work on improving your players and team. Try to achieve perfection (you may as well have high targets) and the results will improve.

The final word on John Wooden, written while he was very much alive, and taken from a fan's online tribute – "Undoubtedly John Wooden was the greatest coach ever in any sport, and is the measuring stick for which all other great coaches of all sports will be measured until the end of time."

SUMMARY

1. Keep it simple – do not confuse people.

2. Be prepared to adjust if necessary – have a Plan B.

3. Concentrate on your own players and team. That is the area over which you have most influence and control.

4. In conjunction with your management team, give some thought to how best to deal with the principal threats posed by your opponents and any possible opportunities which may exist because of a weakness in their team. Try to cover all the bases.

CHAPTER 9

MAD MANAGERS AND TACTICS

"Ordinarily he was insane, but he had lucid moments when he was merely stupid." **Heinrich Heine. German poet**

Gaelic football is evolving at least as much as most other field games. Everyone wanted to play "catch and kick" when this worked for Kerry decades ago. There was a move to a more physical approach when Armagh became successful in recent years. Tyrone introduced a much more fluid game than anything seen previously (notoriously described at the time, as "puke football" by one very famous Kerryman).

Galway, in winning their last two All Irelands combined a short hand-passing game out of defence with early kicked delivery from midfield to their forwards. Kerry under Jack O'Connor introduced the target man full forward, many would say, by accident. This occurred when they were struggling rather surprisingly against Longford and Kieran Donaghy was moved from midfield. However it came about, it worked. The point of all this is that styles vary and change over time.

Indeed the concept of a target-man was far from a new idea. And it was Kerry who had derived most benefit from such a player when Eoin 'Bomber' Liston arrived on the scene in the seventies. What is generally regarded as the best team ever, won its first All Ireland in 1975.

Five of the team were to go on to win eight All Ireland medals but it was not until Eoin Liston arrived into the side, a couple of years after that first win, that they reached their peak. I was interested to see Billy Morgan make this same observation in his autobiography and as player and later manager of deadly rivals Cork, he was well positioned to make such a judgement. Kerry's game changed once Liston arrived. Prior to that they had very skilled but not particularly big forwards. The Bomber could win his own ball, lay it off to one of the others such as Spillane, Egan or Sheehy, or he could use his strength and physique to go it alone. Clearly, Mick O'Dwyer saw the additional attacking options Liston brought to an already exceptional team.

Before addressing in more detail some of the ways a Gaelic football team might be set up, let me tell a story of how not to do it.

This is a true story. A team (The Reds) were to play a big game in the championship. They had a fairly good team with two tall midfielders, both of whom were useful in the air. Their weakness in previous games had been the team's inability to win their share of breaking ball around the centre of the field. Their opposition in this big game was The Blues. The Blues did not have a particularly tall midfield pairing but were very mobile and were excellent at mopping up broken ball in the central area.

Anyone who knew the above details would have been surprised when The Reds took the field with a third tall but slow midfielder lining out in the full-forward line but quickly switching to a third midfielder role. They would have been even more surprised when it became apparent that the defender who followed this third midfielder was tall, quick, and in general a much better player, and while all present could see this, The Reds continued with the plan, while The Blues' defender became the most prominent figure in midfield.

The question, or at least one question is on how many levels did The Red's manager get it wrong?

Firstly, he did not need a third midfielder to win high ball. He should have had an advantage in that respect without tinkering with the team.

If his midfielders were finding it tough, perhaps, as The Blues tried to break as much ball as possible, preventing The Reds getting clean possession, he could have deployed an additional mobile player in the central area to compete for breaking ball. As it was, The Blues kept knocking ball down, the third midfielder was too slow to recover such ball and his man dominated the area.

Once it became clear that the strategy was a disaster (that did not take long) the third midfielder should immediately have been sent back in close to the opposition goal, taking his marker with him.

A friend was having trouble getting to grips with how anyone managing a senior football team could be this stupid. On making enquiries, he discovered that the manager in question was put in contact with an inter-county manager who had a connection to The Reds club. (Someone on the club committee had got to know him before he had become better known as the manager of a county senior football team.) He came to a couple of games and took a few training sessions. The Reds manager was thrilled. In the week before the big game, his new hero suggested, for, no good reason that anyone could explain, that a third midfielder was the way to go. Without questioning why, the Reds manager decided that is what he would do. And that is how the Reds lost a game they should probably have won.

While this story may amuse some – members of The Reds club are clearly exempted from seeing the funny side of it - there are lessons to be learned. To me, the most obvious one is that it is good practice to receive advice. However, acting on that advice requires a degree of calmness, objectivity and judgement which unfortunately for The Reds, were qualities which their manager lacked. It goes back to realising that ultimately, as the manager you must make the hard calls.

By all means listen to every opinion offered but chose what you believe to be the best option in the interests of the team. Be open to suggestions which are made with the best of intentions. But, carefully weigh up any suggested changes before deciding to implement them. Look at what I have previously referred to as the "what ifs". We will play with a third midfielder.

What if the opposition decide to park their spare man in front of their full back line? What if they decide to follow your auxiliary midfielder from his starting position in your forward line? What if they decide to play a third midfielder of their own, someone who has lined out as a full-forward on their team?

It becomes a game of chess. And the manager needs to have thought beyond a single move. The Reds manager took advice from someone who, by definition, had a lot less knowledge of the team than he himself. Having done that, and having changed his selection, he gave no thought to the "what ifs". In this case, what if the opposition follow our man into midfield and begin to dominate? What do we do then? In practice, the answer was "nothing". As a manager, there were those who had long felt he was a little mad, but on this occasion, sadly, he met the description at the top of this chapter which poet Heinrich Heine had applied to a Teutonic autocrat.

Deciding upon actions without considering the consequences and possible reactions is not an unusual phenomenon. Politicians do it all the time. Many bankers and other assorted geniuses used this method to run an entire country onto the rocks. Don't misunderstand me. This is not about being ultra-cautious or even mildly careful. To put it at its simplest, it is just about avoiding being either mad or stupid.

So what options do you have when setting up a team? And does success depend on your ability to come up with an original system or to utilise a particular system which enjoys current popularity?

Elsewhere in this book I have referred to the variety of options available to the manager of a soccer team when it comes to deciding on a system of play or on his team formation. It is hard to imagine that an entire book could be devoted to this subject, and harder still to believe anyone would read it.

In fact, Jonathan Wilson, the football correspondent of the *Financial Times* has written a book called *Inverting the Pyramid*, tracing the history of tactics in football. Not only is it interesting, it is actually an extremely well-written, award-winning effort which traces the history of the game in following the evolution of tactics and how they changed and developed in parts of Europe and South America over the decades. It also offers fascinating insight into the evolution of soccer. With in-depth analysis of the thinking of several of the top football managers, it concludes by explaining how certain internationally known players have been unable to adapt to a changing game and how this has impacted on their careers and on their teams.

Two of the best most insightful examples outline how Claude Makelele was effective at a particular point but how his attributes are no longer sufficient at the very top, and how Michael Owen, injury notwithstanding, became an obsolete type of player whom no Champions League team would sign as he left Real Madrid. The point being made was that the game has evolved and a more flexible player is needed at the very top – put simply, as a player, being able to do just one thing, albeit, being able to do it really well, is no longer enough.

No such work exists for Gaelic football and I believe the time may not yet have arrived for such a work. It would be my, perhaps slightly cynical, contention that the only significant change in the first century of Gaelic football was the change at the start of each half which went from the ball being thrown in to fourteen outfield players from either side, with ensuing chaos, to the present two from each side system.

The old joke about the English soccer manager being so dumb he thought tactics were peppermint sweets might well have been applied to Gaelic football for most of that first century of competition. Has the arrival on the scene of "the manager" brought about the introduction and variation on tactics? It would seem so. The first high profile managers were Mick O'Dwyer and Kevin Heffernan, and the latter was certainly the thinking man's tactician.

The first successful deployment of someone nominally selected in a full forward line but playing elsewhere was when Heffernan used Bobby Doyle in a roving role. The increase in hand-passing is also generally attributed to managers seeking to build from the back, retaining possession for as long as possible.

Sweepers and three-man midfields became more widespread in the eighties and nineties. The evolution in the first decade of this century is, for want of a better term, the homogenisation of wing backs and wing forwards. This coincides with a greater emphasis on defending from the front. Essentially, forwards used to attack and defenders used to defend. Midfielders caught high ball and linked the two sectors. That was when life was simple.

Now, forwards are expected to be able to tackle. Defenders finding themselves upfield are expected to be able to take a score if the opportunity arises. And the midfielders and forwards, especially wing forwards, are expected to cover for the attacking defender. There was a time when a defender finding himself in attack would have been expected to boot the ball somewhere towards the corner flag. Anything approaching a score would have been regarded with awe or as a complete fluke. Not anymore.

To play the modern game, even at club level, a high degree of fitness is required. The amount of ground covered by players is greater than ever. A concentration on short hand passing has been the biggest factor. The consequent unwillingness to kick long – or as it is perceived – to risk losing possession, has, in turn, led directly to a drop in the standard of long kicking. So it really is "chicken and egg".

We hand pass more and more and as a result become a bit better at that. We kick less and less so the standard drops. And as the standard drops, players are further discouraged, by both their own poor ability and the manager's concerns about losing possession, from even attempting to kick long if the short hand pass is an option.

Anyone who has worked with Gaelic football teams will tell you that any system you deploy will depend on the players available to you. For this reason it is impossible to say, "you should do this" or "you should do that" without getting to know what playing resources you have at your disposal.

I have deployed a key player, with high levels of fitness and energy, in a free role, selecting him in the full forward line and allowing him wander between half back and half forward, taking the occasional break back in the full forward line. I have played with a physically stronger but less energetic player in a straight three-man midfield. I have worked with a manager who believed in playing with only four forwards, set up in two lines of two.

The two players taken out played as a sweeper and as a third midfielder. It was a very negative system whose objective, someone once said, was to win by four points to three. I have worked with another manager whose philosophy could be summarised in three words – attack, attack, attack. It was much more fun with that last manager. No matter where you got the ball you were to start building an attack. We didn't win every game but the players enjoyed it, and that is no bad thing.

Sometimes a system or method will evolve. Your big full forward may make deliberation unnecessary as you opt to hit him with as much long ball as possible. Your lack of such a player will eliminate the possibility of kicking in high ball. The basic principle should be to play your best forwards, those most accurate, as near to the opposition goals as possible. If you have more than three such players, the world is yours. Even three with an ability to get scores is exceptional in most club teams these days.

The days when you could have a full-back line of big, strong, slow lads are also well gone. Nowadays, your defenders need to be quick and mobile. There is a time for experimentation and there is a point at which the experiments must stop or it just becomes tinkering. Use the time well. Try out a system which you consider might suit your players. You have chosen selectors and a coach. Discuss the possibilities and use the early days to experiment.

One thing well worth considering is positioning or re-positioning of players. Never assume that all players are in their best positions or roles. I have seen some great examples of players being successfully redeployed to parts of the field which had been alien to them and where they would never have dreamt of playing.

The most recent example is where the manager of one of the top four counties in the country has positioned a player at half back during the early season experimental stage. This player has always been a forward and is now 23 or 24 years of age. But, I believe the manager is absolutely correct to try this. And he is showing great imagination in doing so. If it does not work out the player can revert to competing for a place in a very good forward line, and with no shame attached to him for trying this out.

If it does work, the manager has an experienced, All - Ireland winning player, with pace to burn and years of football ahead of him. He is clearly concerned that not all his existing half back options give him that pace or those years of football. Therefore, in my opinion, this is a win-win trial. It is something from which many club managers can learn. When my business involved manufacturing, we had a saying that "we do this because we always did this". The idea is to break away from that type of thinking. There was always a way to improve methods and efficiencies once some degree of imagination was applied, once people could be got out of rigid thinking.

So show some imagination in trying out different tactical approaches or in positioning players. But limit the time for experiments. With your management team, set a deadline for experimentation and tinkering. When you are trying out a system in pre-season, it can prove useful to play challenge or friendly games against teams which may not be of your standard. If you are the better team, it gives you a good chance to develop and hone your chosen method. If you believe in anything in life, in this case, if you believe in a particular method or system, then get everybody on board and persevere with it.

SUMMARY

1. Do not get bogged down over tactics.

2. There is no "right" system.

3. How your team is set up will be governed by the type of players available to you.

4. Utilise the expertise of your management team in deciding on tactics.

5. Experiment early in the season and then, based on evidence and consultation, make a decision.

6. Do not be influenced by people who know less about your squad of players than you do.

CHAPTER 10

DISCIPLINE AND REFEREES

'I'm not a bastard...'

"Discipline is remembering what you want."
David Campbell, Canadian politician

Of all the quotations or axioms I have come across, this is probably the line that impresses me most because it sums everything up in a short six words. If players fully understand and remember what they want they will adjust their behaviour so as not to do anything that deprives them of that prize.

Discipline involves more than players simply behaving themselves on the field. We have already referred to a situation where players broke an agreed drinking ban rule and had to take the consequences. However let us first deal with discipline on the field.

It was my first game in charge of the team. It was a senior league fixture on our opponents ground. Both management teams were on the same sideline in close proximity to an incident wherein our full forward fouled the opposing full back. The referee blew for a free out to the home team. As the players were moving back, the full back who had been awarded the free had some words with the referee over the precise position from which the kick should be taken.

Out of earshot one word borrowed another when

suddenly the referee decided he had heard enough and our hosts would forfeit their free. The ref would instead throw the ball in between a player from each side. The ref called for the ball and came close to where we were positioned on the sideline. Two players were lined up to contest the throw-in when the referee, ball in hand, turned to the full back who had given him an earful, and from 25 metres uttered the immortal line, "and by the way, I'm not a bastard" – he then shaped to throw the ball up before completing his sentence "ye bollix ye". You couldn't make it up.

It might be advisable to have your players assume that the average referee is unlikely to react along these lines when his heredity has been called into question.

Most are likely to apply the rules instead – not surprisingly – and cancel the free while booking the player foolishly questioning the ref's parentage.

Cultures vary across different sports. Rugby is famously disciplined in the sense that players accept referees' decisions no matter how much they may feel aggrieved by the decision. From a young age and particularly in schools rugby, they are drilled in accepting decisions no matter how stupid or unjust. In soccer there is more of a tendency to question decisions but yellow cards are frequently the response and those cards can have a cumulative effect leading to suspensions.

There is a story about John Wooden when UCLA were at their peak and winning National basketball Championships. One of his top players was a bit of a maverick and returned to college after the summer break, with long hair and a beard. Now Wooden had strict rules in relation to hair. They were not authoritarian for the sake of it. His reasoning was that a player sweats during the course of a game.

A player with long hair and/or a beard would be likely to run his hands through his hair resulting in wet hands and a higher chance of the ball slipping from his grip. So Wooden asked his player to please remember the rules and return next day with short hair and no beard. Next day at practice, the player duly appeared still unshorn of hair or beard.

He approached Wooden and told him how he valued individuality and felt he should be true to himself and his principles that he was still totally committed to the team but that his individual rights were something he treasured and he was sure the coach would agree. Wooden told him he completely respected and understood the player's wish to be an individual and went along those lines before concluding with the words: "We are sure going to miss you." Next day he had a clean-shaven player with hair cut like the rest of the squad.

DISCIPLINE IN GAMES

In the world of the GAA, decisions which are even slightly dubious are almost invariably questioned. The first sanction for such questioning of authority is loss of ground. In Gaelic football, a player arguing the awarding of a free against him will forfeit thirteen metres, as the referee quite correctly moves the ball forward. A player foolish enough to follow the route of the above-mentioned argumentative full-back will have his free forfeited and the ball thrown in, and, usually he will receive a yellow card rather than simply being called a "bollix".

In Gaelic football, the loss of 13 metres can be devastating. As a group, referees are not the best judges of distance and the supposed 13 metres is often closer to 20 metres. This, I believe, is the logical and fairly predictable response from someone whose authority has been questioned, often in an unpleasant way. Critically for the offending team, their opponent's free kick is moved to a more advantageous position, often bringing it from outside scoring range in to where it can be converted, or from a difficult angle to where now it would be harder for the kicker to miss.

As manager it is your task to see to it that your players fully understand the consequences and keep their mouths shut, accepting decisions regardless of how unjustified they feel those decisions may be. It is not an easy task but one good way to get the message home is to referee practice games in training. During those games you should deliberately give wrong decisions and deal with the uproar that follows.

You can even tell your players in advance that you will be giving these wrong decisions. It does not prevent them responding, at least initially. Over time they begin to get it, and are less likely to give up the vital ground in games. They must be forced to admit they have never known a referee to change a decision when asked nicely, let alone when subjected to abuse. Come to think of it, when was the last time you heard a referee asked anything nicely?

There was a time when "one in, all in" was the prevailing philosophy in GAA games. It is the type of "philosophy" which is applied in Aussie rules also. The 1996 All Ireland football Final replay between Meath and Mayo is one of the more memorable examples. However, over time, discipline has generally improved with greater powers vested in linesmen coupled with neutral umpires in championship games.

In most cases indiscipline is punished these days. Therefore you will not want players becoming involved in brawls and risking suspensions. So discipline needs to be preached with the consequences of indiscipline discussed and understood by all members of your playing panel.

To summarise, the team cannot afford to give up ground by arguing decisions. Giving up ground very often amounts to giving up scores. Neither does the team need to lose players on two yellow cards or worse still on straight red cards, for offences leading to suspensions. Football, hurling and most other team field sports involve physical contact. No one wants to see players bullied or cowed into submission. But players must be taught that in the long run, discipline will stand to them and more importantly, to their team. In rugby, we frequently see indiscipline lead to penalties. Again, work has to be done to ensure maximum levels of concentration and discipline at all times.

The final argument in favour of having a highly disciplined team with each member in full control of his/her temper is that anything less leads to a disruption in concentration. A player becoming involved with the referee or with another official is not concentrating on what should be the priority, winning the next ball and getting the next score.

By the same token, all members of team management must exercise discipline in their behaviour. There is little point in calling on players to show restraint if any one member of management is likely to behave otherwise. It has long been a feature of GAA games that referees come in for abuse from team mentors. If you wish to engender the necessary high levels of discipline in your team, avoid having a management member who cannot behave as you would wish. Again, you are the manager; you are in charge; so you must make sure everyone understands the standards you wish to apply.

DISCIPLINE IN GENERAL

Discipline has more than one meaning or interpretation. It could be argued, and I would certainly do so, that good habits are the basis of the type of disciplined approach required of your team. To me, discipline begins with all players turning up on time for training, for matches and for meetings. If the requirement is to be on the training ground at 7.30 then it is not good practice to have players traipsing on to the field ten or fifteen minutes later when the warm-up is well underway. Having the correct equipment and gear (or the part of their own gear for which players themselves are responsible such as shorts and socks), is part of the business of having good habits, or being disciplined.

It must be said that in reference to training sessions, these should be organised in a manner that shows discipline on the part of management. If cones or poles are required for drills they should be in place before the session starts, i.e. before the players arrive onto the field. If instructions are to be given, this should be done quickly, preferably before the players come out of the dressing rooms. If bibs are to be allocated, this should be done in advance of leaving the changing rooms or at the very beginning rather than in confusion during what becomes an unnecessarily long break. If the spectrum extends from totally disciplined and professional to shambolic at the other extreme, you know where you want to be.

SUMMARY

1. Discipline has more than one facet.

2. Discipline covers a mentality among the players that affects their entire approach, to training, to general preparation and to playing. It is not simply their relationship with referees or other officials.

3. If discipline is not good, you have no chance.

4. Discipline which has to be imposed should be imposed fairly – but firmly.

CHAPTER 11

LEADERSHIP, MANAGEMENT AND MOTIVATION

"Management is nothing more than motivating other people." Lee Iacocca, president Chrysler corporation

All of which brings us to look at the different types of managers. As I have already pointed out, the titles vary from sport to sport. Australian Rules, like rugby football, refers to the person in charge as the coach but to all intents and purposes the role is that of manager in the sense that we apply it to most field games.

The *Aussie Rules Official Manual* quite interestingly describes the different types of coach/manager, the distinguishing characteristics and the implications of having a person of each type in charge of a team. They are listed as:

AUTHORITARIAN
- Strong disciplinarian.
- Well-organised.
- Good team spirit when winning.
- Dissension when losing.
- May be feared or disliked.
- (Don't you love that line - "good team spirit – when winning")

BUSINESS-LIKE
- Intelligent, logical approach.
- Well-planned and organised. Up to date with new techniques.
- Expects 100 per cent effort all the time.
- May set goals too high for some team members.

NICE GUY
- Well liked.
- Players sometimes take advantage of his co-operative nature.

INTENSE
- Emphasises winning.
- High anxiety often transmitted to players.

EASY-GOING
- Very casual. Gives impression of not taking the game seriously.
- May not be prepared to drive team.
- Well-liked but may seem to be inadequate in some situations.

Undoubtedly, there will be attributes here which will strike a chord. The lesson I take from this list of prototypes is that the ideal manager will require some elements of the authoritarian, business-like and nice guy descriptions. Once again, the word "balance" arises. In management, as in all walks of life where the objective is to achieve something positive, zealots are to be avoided as are the totally laid back. Can you distinguish between management and leadership? Which do you wish to become, a manager or a leader? In the world of Business Management training, leadership is defined as both a process and a property. As a process it involves the use of non-coercive influence while as a property it is the set of characteristics attributed to a person who is said to use influence successfully. You will note from this that while someone may be described as a manager, they will not be considered a leader if their methodology is to rule by fear.

This very point may explain some high-profile failures especially in soccer. Management, on the other hand, is regarded as controlling and problem solving. So management is seen as more technical and functional than leadership which involves the emotions to quite a high degree.

If a manager is not connecting with players on an emotional level, then the influence over the players will not be the same. Do not be misled into thinking that reference to an emotional connection means the player and manager must like or love each other.

I recall an excellent documentary programme on Brian Clough's management career. When Clough managed both Derby County and Nottingham Forest to league titles he became only the second manager in the history of English football to win titles with different teams. What was miraculous was that neither was a big or even slightly fashionable club. Also, his teams included several players which the prevailing wisdom believed could not possibly be in championship winning teams. Most notable of these was John McGovern, who won a League medal with Derby County and went on the captain Forest through their great successes, and who was not highly-rated by many so-called experts. A vital component in both teams, McGovern was interviewed for this documentary programme and asked his opinions on Clough and their relationship. The interviewer was taken aback when McGovern made it quite clear he and Clough had not been friends.

He went so far as to suggest he would never have had him as a friend, that as a person he did not have any great love for Clough, but, and this is the critical tribute to Clough's leadership, McGovern said, "I'd have gone absolutely anywhere to play for him." I found this akin to the type of comments made by troops about the great generals who led them into battle, the kind of people whose leadership attributes were legendary.

John P Kotter of Harvard says, "leadership complements management; it doesn't replace it." It may be concluded that in a perfect world, the manager can deal with all the nuts and bolts issues while providing the inspiration to lift the team to unprecedented heights.

It would appear that, in the sporting context, strong qualities of leadership are essential for ultimate success. It is a world that is and always has been blessed with great leaders, on and off the field of play. When we think of leaders in sport we think perhaps of other football managers such as Matt Busby, Jock Stein, Bill Shankly, Bob Paisley and in the modern era Alex Ferguson, Pep Guardiola and Jose Mourinho. All were/are strong individuals whose leadership qualities were evident.

In business we have seen the success of great leaders such as Bill Gates at Microsoft and Steve Jobs at Apple and in Ireland, Ryanair boss Michael O'Leary. US basketball in particular has offered great leaders such as Phil Jackson, Rick Pitino and the most revered of all, John Wooden.

Irish sport has given us Declan Kidney, and several truly great manager/leaders in Gaelic games. What is fascinating about these people is they have a wide range of personalities. As loud and forceful as Clough, Mourinho and O'Leary have been, Bob Paisley, Matt Busby and Bill Gates could hardly be called extrovert attention-seekers.

When motivation is mentioned in the sporting context, it is clear that leadership, if it means influencing on an emotional level, means inspiring or motivating. In its broadest sense, motivation is dealt with in social and business studies where the famous "Maslow's Hierarchy of Needs" is often applied. This is simply a description of the various levels of needs of the average human being and how the needs change as each one in turn is satisfied. In sport, this changing of needs or this motivation which changes over time, explains why it is difficult or impossible to keep a winning team at the top, indefinitely.

Their motivation has changed as their need to win has been fulfilled – put simply – the hunger goes.

In terms of your own approach to motivation, much of what you should do is in line with the other aspects of the management task, follow your instinct and use common sense.

A structure called "The 4R's of Motivation" may be of help.

Reason: Explain the "why" in your policies and practices

Responsibility: Give people the power to act

Relationship: Allow interaction between the players

Recognition: Give specific feedback which is valued by the players

There is a piece on motivation, called "The Carrot is Mightier Than a Stick" which quotes John Wooden.

"Carrots come in many forms. However, I believe the strongest and most meaningful motivators are not necessarily the materialistic, but the intangible. In this regard, there is perhaps no better carrot than approval from someone you truly respect, whose recognition you seek.....importantly, sincere approval instils pride. Punishment invokes fear. I wanted a team whose members were filled with pride, not fear."

I have described leadership as having an emotional aspect as opposed to the act of managing which is more functional. Lest there be any misunderstanding, where emotions are concerned it is well to realise the difference between controlled emotions or intensity and uncontrolled emotional or mercurial behaviour which will not help you achieve your goals. Remember: Control your emotions or they will control you. Realise the difference between being intensely committed and being hyper.

SUMMARY

1. Will you be a manager or leader? A manager is very much a technician but you should aspire to be a leader – the best possible type of manager.

2. The difference between leadership and management is explained as: leadership is doing the right thing while management is doing things right.

3. As a leader you will need to provide some spark of inspiration and to connect with players at an emotional level.

4. Respect for the individual should always be incorporated into everything you do and say.

5. Meanwhile, on more mundane matters you will need to be organised in such areas as knowing what equipment and facilities you require.

6. Make sure your players know what is expected of them throughout the season, on and off the field.

7. Only make commitments which you know you can keep.

8. Be clear in your statements so as to avoid misunderstandings.

CHAPTER 12

WAYS TO HELP YOURSELF

"The manager's indecision is final." **Duncan McKenzie, former Leeds United footballer**

BE DECISIVE

In relation to decisions around disciplinary matters:

A. If you make rules you need to apply them.

B. Do not make a rule you may be unprepared to implement.

C. You must be seen to be fair.

D. Be firm but fair and then move on. Do not rejoice or come across all macho because you have been forced to make a tough decision.

E. Above all, make a decision. First get all the facts. Discuss the situation with your management colleagues who will have a viewpoint. Realise that having assembled all the known facts and discussed the matter with those around you a decision must be taken. If you are true to your initial promises, that decision will be taken in the interests of the team.

F. In disciplinary matters do not hold any grudges. Once the matter is dealt with, or in such as the previously mentioned case when the players are re-introduced to the panel, their earlier indiscretions are forgotten and it is a fresh start.

G. Confront problems. Do not let them drag on. The

point of being manager is not that you get the glory when success happens. You must do the unpleasant jobs, especially dealing with indiscipline or telling a committed and loyal player he has been dropped for a big game.

With regard to making decisions, remember you are the manager which is defined as "being in charge".

In terms of decision-making, and it would be good to think all decisions are not about disciplinary matters, you have a management team which you should treat as a resource. The people you have chosen are there to do the work allocated but also to offer their opinions and their advice based on their own skills and experience. The world is full of managers who want to make decisions without first getting all possible information and opinions onto the table.

No one is suggesting, by the way, that it is necessary to agonise over all decisions. Gather the information. Hear what the others believe and then make the decision. Again, if your decision is diametrically opposed to the view of one of your management colleagues, it would help to take that person aside and explain your thinking. Most people in that situation will realise where the buck does stop. If you have a clear understanding with your colleagues, they will all know that in the final analysis it is your call.

Where team sports are concerned many decisions will revolve around team selection, a substitution or a proposed switch during a game. If those selecting the team have taken a little time to look at the "what ifs" in advance, life can be made easier when switches are needed. Very often a player's form or loss of form will present the problem for management. Individuals react differently to being omitted or substituted. Others are watching from the bench and perhaps wondering what it takes for some people to be taken off so they themselves can get their chance to shine.

Having clear policies, communicating them consistently and being consistent in your decision-making are the keys. It is also helpful that players clearly understand that management reserves the right to make substitutions and will always do so with the solitary objective of winning the particular game. They must understand that if a player is considered to be having a bad day, no matter his status or previous record, he will be substituted if that is believed to be of help to the team on the day in question.

It does not mean anyone thinks he has become a bad player or that anyone dislikes him. It is amazing how often this can be spelt out and players with big egos still react badly to being taken off. It is one of the factors that must be made clear from the beginning. You do not want a top player going into a sulk because he/she was having an off-day and was subbed. Neither do you want to leave such a player on the field when they are having a nightmare of a game.

Again, it is about establishing a clear understanding of how things will work. Spell it out. Repeat points as often as you feel necessary. Remember one thing about talking in generalisations to a room full of players; if you are imparting a tough message, most of them will think you are addressing it to someone else. "He's talking disciplinary matters – I'm perfect – it could not be aimed at me." If you assume that is what is going through a number of heads, it might enable you to make the point more clearly and forcefully. Then, when you have to make the tough decision which affects a player, it should not be met with shock and horror.

SUMMARY

1. As with most things in life, there is a balance to decision-making.

2. Hasty decisions are often a prelude to problems.

3. Dithering is not much use either.

4. Get as much information as possible.

5. Consult within the camp, and if necessary outside as well.

6. Then make the decision and stand over it.

BE INQUISITIVE

"I have no particular talent, I am merely inquisitive."
Albert Einstein

Study managers in your chosen sport

Whatever your aspirations as a manager you can learn by studying successful managers in your own sport, in other sports or in other spheres such as business.

Gaelic football has produced several great managers over the years. Seán Boylan and Mickey Harte are two whose achievements impress me greatly. Boylan came from a hurling background and took over Meath when they were at a low ebb, bringing them prolonged success over more than 20 years.

Harte persevered with Tyrone minor (under-18) teams until he realised a burning ambition when leading them to an All Ireland win. Further All Ireland success was achieved at under-21 and finally at senior level when Tyrone achieved the breakthrough in 2003 under his inspired leadership.

There have been many others from, Mick O'Dwyer and Jack O'Connor of Kerry to Billy Morgan who shares with Eugene McGee and Joe Kernan the achievement of All Ireland management success with both club and county.

Hurling has given us Brian Cody, Donal O'Grady and the inimitable Michael 'Babs' Keating. Liam Sheedy's achievement in taking Tipperary to All Ireland success in 2010 puts him right up there with the best managers.

I make this contention because of the comprehensive manner in which his team won that final.

Yet they were only a point ahead as time ran out on Galway in a thrilling quarter-final. It's a fine line alright between success and failure. His decision to stand down immediately after the final win reflects on the difficulty of devoting the necessary time and energy to such an intense job while also having to work for a living in the "real world".

It is clear from reading biographies on Boylan and Harte that each of these men has an innate respect for people. Their concerns would have been primarily for their players whom they treated with great respect. But neither was inhibited when it came to taking tough decisions.

They took those decisions in the interests of the team, which was above everything else to them and they conveyed bad news to players in a most humane and considerate way. Reading about these very successful and very modest men, one gets a great insight into how they functioned. Hard work and intelligent application were the basis of their success.

There is a parallel in the situations they found themselves in when seeking their first All Irelands as managers. Neither had been a successful inter county footballer. Meath had been out of the limelight when Seán Boylan took over the team. Tyrone had never enjoyed senior All Ireland success when Mickey Harte became manager.

So both men had to persuade players that they could

win All Irelands. As Boylan says "there's always a chance" and he uses that phrase not just about winning after continuous failure but even in a game where things are going badly, his belief conveyed to his teams is, "keep working – there's always a chance". And he has been vindicated so often in that belief as his teams were never beaten until the final whistle and regularly salvaged what seemed lost causes.

Study managers in other sports

There are numerous books on the great football managers from Shankly and Clough to Capello and Trapattoni and, of course, Alex Ferguson. There are biographies or autobiographies on great American coaches from John Wooden (a hero of Mickey Harte's) to Rick Pitino and Billy Beane. Nearer to home, there can be few managers as successful as Declan Kidney. His methods are worth studying. I know his official title is coach but he is every bit as much a manager as most managers in other sports. Ian McGeechan's story is also well worth studying.

Fabio Capello is one of the world's most successful managers, whatever the outcome of his time with the England football team. He has a fantastic record in Italy. He has twice gone to Spain to manage Real Madrid, each time for one year and 10 years apart. Each time they had been struggling unsuccessfully and each time he led them to the league title.

David James, the experienced England goalkeeper, was asked the interesting question. "How does his style of management differ to the other England managers you've worked under"? His reply tells a lot: "He's straight to the point and doesn't take any messing. He knows what he wants and is not afraid to say it and I think that ultimately earns the respect of the squad. He's not afraid to say it straight and it's never personal. If he sees something good he'll say it there and then, doesn't matter who you are. That commands a lot of respect from players because there is no ambiguity."

This description is worth analysing:
- Straight to the point.
- Does not take any messing.
- Says things straight out.
- It is never personal.
- If he sees something good he will say it.
- No ambiguity.

Any manager seeking to develop and improve could do a lot worse than follow these principles. Straight-forward honesty, praise and encouragement for worthy efforts, intolerance of messing and avoidance of ambiguity go a long way towards getting the respect a manager needs if he is to succeed.

And while your ambition may not extend to managing Real Madrid, while that task may be much more onerous, the basic principles of good management are pretty much the same whether you or on £6m per annum or managing a club team for the sheer challenge and enjoyment of trying to achieve success at local level. The extent to which successful managers exhibit similar traits, regardless of nationality or the particular game tells us something about succeeding as a manager.

Take the following example: Seán Boylan in his autobiography is quoted when he first took over the Meath football team, "I would have to get their fitness levels up; get them to believe in themselves and get them used to winning." NBA All Star Mark Jackson talks about the great basketball coach Rick Pitino: "His greatest strength is making people believe in themselves and in each other." Interestingly, when discussing Mick O'Dwyer's methods with players who have played under him, the one common point they all make is his ability to make you believe in yourself.

So if "making people believe in themselves and each other" is good enough for Seán Boylan, Mick O'Dwyer and Rick Pitino, it would be foolish to underestimate the potential gains from a positive approach. To get to that stage it is necessary to create the environment in which players can see the possibility of achieving their potential.

The Rick Pitino autobiography, *Rebound Rules* has some very enlightening observations:

Pitino on statistics – the importance of using the data you are generating: "If we were getting 35 deflections per game, we tried to get closer to 40. We would try to overcome the loss of overwhelming talent with an increase in hustle – and deflections are the clearest way to gauge that vague dynamic. If your players are active – in the face of the man they're guarding, waving their hands, sprinting back to help on defence – they're going to get their hands on the ball. When you demand great effort from your players, that's the one place it will show up statistically. That's why we assign an assistant coach to do nothing but chart deflections, by player, for every game. Certain statistics don't lie, and they pan out over a period of time."

Pitino quotes a man called Geoffrey Colvin writing in *Money* magazine (top managers are looking at other fields for inspiration,) Colvin talks about deliberate practice: "Simply hitting a bucket of balls is not deliberate practice, which is why most golfers don't get better. Hitting an eight-iron 300 times with a goal of leaving the ball within 20 feet of the pin 80 per cent of the time, continually observing results and making appropriate adjustments, and doing that for hours every day – that's deliberate practice."

Anyone old enough with an interest in American football (gridiron) will recall the era when the game was dominated by the San Francisco 49ers led by brilliant quarter-back, Joe Montana. Montana's target for the crucial throws leading to game-breaking scores was invariably his great wide receiver, Jerry Rice. This is a piece describing Rice's off-season workout and attributing his longevity to his incredible work ethic: "Rice's six-day-a-week workout is divided into two parts: two hours of cardiovascular work in the morning and three hours of strength training each afternoon.

"Early in the off-season, the a.m. segment consists of a five-mile trail run near San Carlos on a torturous course called simply, The Hill. But since five vertical miles can hardly be considered a workout, he pauses on the steepest section to do a series of ten 40-metre uphill sprints. As the season approaches, however, Rice knows it's time to start conserving energy – so he forgoes The Hill and instead merely does a couple of sprints: six 100 yarders, six 80s, six 60s, six 40s, six 20s and sixteen 10s, with no rest between sprints and two-and-a-half minutes between sets.

"For the p.m. sessions he alternates between upper-body and lower- body days. But no matter which half of his body he's working on, the volume is always the same: three sets of ten reps of 21 different exercises. Yes, your calculator is right: that's 630 repetitions a day."

Now, I realise Jerry Rice was a professional and you will be dealing with amateur players. It is, however, worth remembering and worth reminding your players that there is no substitute for hard work. And remember deliberate practice beats the other kind every time.

Look outside sport

Bestselling author Malcolm Gladwell (*The Tipping Point*, *Blink* and *Outliers*) writes quirky books with an interesting take on aspects of life and business. In *Outliers* he has a piece on the 10,000 hour rule. His point is that it takes 10,000 hours of practice – from birth – to achieve perfection. He applies this to various examples such as

The Beatles, counting all those hours they practised and played in Hamburg, before hitting the top.

He contends that all Chess Grand Masters with the single exception of Bobby Fischer had actually played that many hours before achieving the ultimate level – being rated Grand Master. If one tries to apply a 10,000-hour rule to Gaelic football, the likely conclusion is that players peak at 30 or older. It doesn't quite work out but the key point is that in order to succeed players must apply themselves over time.

My point in quoting such diverse examples to you is that, if you do have a burning ambition to succeed, firstly you need to be aware that only serious hard work will bring about success and secondly, this is something which you must convey to your players while leading by example.

In an article in the *Harvard Business Review*, coach and management consultant, Carol Walker, had this to say about rookie managers: "Many rookie managers fail to grasp how their roles have changed: that their jobs are no longer about personal achievement but about enabling others to achieve, that sometimes driving the bus means taking a back seat, and that building a team is often more important than cutting a deal." She goes on to address the five problem areas that rookie managers typically face: delegating, getting support from senior staffers, projecting confidence, thinking strategically and giving feedback."

Once again the similarities between the description of

a business environment and a sports situation are very valid. A new and inexperienced manager of the football team must realise any previous role such as player, is now in the past. Delegating has been well addressed in terms of the management team, obtaining support of senior staffers can be compared with having support of the management team and the senior players.

I would suggest here that the support will come in that order, first the fellow members of management whose very support will help enlist the support of the more senior players. Projecting confidence is admittedly easier for someone who has experience but the more organised the management set-up, the more the small details have been sorted, the clearer the vision, then the easier it becomes to have confidence and to project confidence. Strategic thinking and planning has also been addressed and feedback is as important in team sports as it is in business. It's what you will get informally during a season, but get it formally at those no-holds-barred meetings to review games.

A final word on learning is that there are sporting contests virtually every week of the year. They are on television and they are reported in the newspapers. I would say there is never a week when some lesson cannot be taken from a game, its outcome or the reasons why a particular team won. You simply have to look for it. A random example is one which I have used in trying to get forwards to make intelligent runs when they see their own half-backs or midfielders carrying the ball up the field.

There is a tendency to run in a straight line towards the teammate with the ball. Their marker will almost always be in close attention, making the pass a difficult one as it has only a narrow corridor to travel because it must land just short of the receiving forward. I cited American football games where the quarterback has the ball and is seeking a target at which he can throw. The receivers (forwards) will always start with a fake run to the left or right, wrong-footing the defender, before timing a run to the other side and giving the quarterback an area to which he can attempt to throw the pass.

The same type of movement by a Gaelic football forward gives his team mate a much bigger target area into which to kick a diagonal pass.

SUMMARY
1. Be inquisitive about how managers of teams succeed.
2. Look at attitudes of successful people, present and past.
3. Never underestimate the need for hard work by players and management.
4. Learn from what is happening in sport at this moment.

CHAPTER 13

THE P.I.S.S. PRINCIPLE
'Persistence, Integrity, Sincerity, Skill'

"Victory belongs to the most persevering." **Napoleon**

He lost eight elections. He twice failed in business. His fiancée died. He had a nervous breakdown. Showing extraordinary persistence, he ran for president. Not only was he elected but he came to be regarded as a truly great president who presided at a most difficult time – The American Civil War.

His name was Abraham Lincoln.

●

He has been a professional soccer player all his life. At age 31 he had never played in a team that won a major competition, so he had never won a medal of note. By 2010, at 37, he holds five Serie A Italian championship medals. He has three Italian Cup Medals and four Italian Supercup medals. He has a Champions League medal. Not only does he have a World Cup winners medal, he scored the goal that enabled Italy to go into extra-time and win. He scored in the eventual penalty shoot-out. Before that, memorably, he was head-butted by Zinedine Zidane.

His name is Marco Materazzi.

●

The more one reads about people who have been successful in life and more especially in sport, the more the words "hard work" and "persistence" arise. In the first job I ever held, I was quickly made aware that the four attributes, persistence, integrity, sincerity and skill, were those of the perfect salesman. This was the Proctor and Gamble mantra. I learned later that these attributes could be applied to many other functions besides selling. Also the acronym was easily remembered.

Let's apply those characteristics to the club manager.

1. Persistence

To quote Bill Bradley, Hall of Fame basketball player and former US senator: "Ambition is the path to success. Persistence is the vehicle you arrive in". Do not be deterred if you fail to achieve instant success. Whether over the course of a game, a season or a career, if things are not working out as well as you hoped, never lose hope, never give up. The great tennis player Bjorn Borg was asked which quality was his greatest asset. He unhesitatingly said it was persistence – "my greatest point is my persistence. I never give up in a match. However down I am, I fight until the last ball. My list of matches shows that I have turned a great many so-called irretrievable defeats into victories." Remember Seán Boylan's words "there's always a chance." Being persistent means not giving in to setbacks or defeats but learning from adversity. The most useful piece of advice I ever received was : "It's not what happens to you in life, it's what you do about it."

2. Integrity

I have outlined the need to communicate clearly with your players. In referring to the Psychological Contract I make it clear that it is a two-sided deal. You are outlining what is expected of the players but critically, you are also explaining what expectations the players ought to have in terms of how they will be treated. Your reputation for integrity will depend on how well you keep your word on those commitments. And from your point of view it is worth remembering, it is far easier to take a player to task for not keeping his/her side of the bargain when, quite clearly, you have kept up your undertakings.

3. Sincerity

The entertainer and humorist George Burns is credited with the line, in commenting on how to make it in Hollywood. "Sincerity, if you can fake that, you've got it made." In the real world, people tend to see through fakes a little bit easier than in Hollywood. Be yourself, be honest and you will find people respond well to that.

4. Skill

Skill is something which has to be developed by work and by practice. This is a very good reason why people without any training should not be parachuted into jobs which require skills. It is the argument in favour of not trying to start at the top but to take steps in management one-at-a-time. Walk first – learn to coach - with an under-age or junior team, or become an apprentice member of a management team. Develop the necessary skills before attempting something more challenging like the senior team, the county team or perhaps that £6m job in London, Milan or Madrid.

SUMMARY
1. Your behaviour should be the guideline for your team.
2. You have to preach the mantra of never giving up.
3. You have to set standards of integrity and sincerity.
4. Finally, you must see that players are helped to develop their skills.

CHAPTER 14
SPORTS PSYCHOLOGY

"90% of the game is half-mental." **Yogi Berra.**
New York Yankees player, manager and legend

We have all heard comments to the effect that the most important five or six inches in the game is the five or six inches between the ears of each player. Indeed, the golfer Bobby Jones is quoted as having said: "Competitive golf is played mainly on a five-and-half-inch course: the space between your ears". We have heard of players being "up for it" or a player or team being "totally focused". None of these references has any connection to physical fitness or tactical planning but relate entirely to mental attitude and preparation.

One of the attributes said to be required in an Australian Rules coach is the capability to practice sports psychology. It is not uncommon to hear a club manager say: "You would want to be a psychologist to understand some of those lads."

It is said half-jokingly and usually during a rant which includes some of the other alleged requirements such as being a nanny, wet-nurse, mother, to some of the more childish members of the team. So much of what some of the successful managers already do could easily be described as psychology.

They may not have the formal qualifications but they

spend a good deal of time trying to work on the minds of their players. In Jose Mourinho's case the time is often spent working on the minds of the opposition players and managers. Mental preparation is widely recognised now. In the 21st century few would argue that it does not form a serious element within the overall preparation of a sports team.

Frequently we read of individuals such as tennis players, golfers or athletes using sports psychologists. At higher levels than amateur club teams, it is quite common to have a sports psychologist work with the team, becoming an important and ever-present member of management.

This development is less common at club level, mainly for the usual reasons such as cost and availability of a suitably qualified person. Also, there may be a certain degree of scepticism and misunderstanding of what may be possible or how sports psychology could help.

The science is not a new one. Indeed in their book *Pure Sport – Practical Sports Psychology*, John Kremer and Aidan P Moran trace sports psychology back to the ancient Greeks. So the question for someone managing a club team is "does it have a role to play?" and how can the manager avail of the services of a sports psychologist? To begin with, anything that might help improve a team should be considered.

The finances of a club may not allow a long–term involvement of a qualified sports psychologist but that does not rule out some involvement. The best starting position is to talk to such a person. I have brought one in to talk to a team early in the season. Prior to doing so, I went through a briefing session with the person in question.

They asked me a number of questions about the characteristics of the team and the issues that caused me the greatest concern. They came in on a one-off basis and dispensed some very useful advice. There was a cost and the club was not particularly well resourced but I believe we got value for money and that the session was beneficial to some players and therefore to the team. Such a person is trained to identify areas for improvement.

You will find they already know the kind of concerns the manager will have. If everyone agrees that mental preparation is important, that getting through to their heads is vital, it seems to me it logically follows that any expertise which can be brought to that task can only be helpful. Sports psychologists deal with goal setting, with overcoming fears, with becoming more focused, with the mental side of preparation.

They deal with imagining or visualisation, something associated with individual sports people such as swimmers or golfers but something increasingly used by team players and worthy of exploration by any manager seeking an edge.

CONSISTENCY

Of all the traits witnessed in the best teams, consistency is the most admired and probably the most difficult to achieve. As a manager, consistency (providing this means consistently excellent) is what you would desire in your team. Bear this in mind as you set about your job because the first step in achieving it is for you to behave consistently.

The New York Yankees World Series winning manager, Joe Torre, summed it up well when he said: "Whatever your job, consistency is the hallmark. It's much more important than doing something spectacular just once. Do your job consistently and you will be considered good." For a player or indeed a team to show consistency, there is a need to learn how to cope when things are not going well.

There is a need to learn not to panic but to stick at the task and try to play out of the slump. This is easier said than done but it was a hallmark of great tennis players such as Chris Evert and golfers like Jack Nicklaus. For the manager it is also a case of not panicking, not showing weakness but bringing calmness and concentration to the difficult moments.

It is a recognised fact that major finals in team sports are more likely to disappoint than enthral. The single biggest reason is the tension and anxiety among the participants. This is where the ultimate consistency comes in: the team which can play as well on all occasions regardless of the size of the crowd or what rewards are at stake, is the team that is most likely to take the big prizes. The Spain team that won the 2010 World Cup in South Africa is as good an example as one could find.

Despite meeting different types of opponents, some of whom allowed them play their close passing game and some who most certainly did not, they stuck to their plan, they played the same type of game, no matter how difficult that became. In the final, it became as difficult as they could have imagined in their worst nightmares, as they encountered rough and rugged spoiling tactics from a less skilful but physically strong team.

Spain's triumph was a triumph for consistency. It was consistency of belief and of execution. By not allowing themselves to be blown off course, by not deviating from their attempts to play their normal game, they earned worldwide admiration as well as the ultimate prize, the World Cup.

GOAL-SETTING

Having taken responsibility for the club team and having set out the areas covered by the Psychological Contract, now it would be useful to agree the objectives or goals for the team. You will need some discussion on "what happened last year" or maybe over the last three years. This should not become a forum for criticising the previous management team.

Whatever their deficiencies and however obvious these may be do not go there. Concentrate on factors which can be improved or problems which can be eliminated. You then get to setting agreed goals for the team. It is useful to have a major long-term goal as well as short-term goals.

I know "short-term goal" in some cases might be "win a game" but it should be possible to establish realistic goals based on past performance, any changes that may have occurred, such as in playing personnel and the improvements which the panel of players believes are achievable.

Goal setting is very much a part of the corporate business world. The broad view is that goals should be "challenging but not unreasonably difficult." However, Tom Peters the author of "In Search of Excellence" refers to "stretch goals", meaning extremely ambitious goals, which he favours.

However, the problem with setting objectives which are over-ambitious is that people tend to become de-motivated when these goals are not reached. Again, in business, it is recommended that goals should have a defined time period within which they are to be reached and that goals should be linked to rewards.

Translating those views into the world of sports, and in this case club team management, setting defined time periods should not be a problem. In amateur sports the concept of rewards will differ from that of the corporate sector. However, the rewards here are just as tangible. For bonuses and salary increases read improvement and winning of competitions and trophies.

If we take on board the defined time period concept, this fits well with the view, described elsewhere, that the first step in bringing about change is to instil a sense of urgency. If goals are set for short-term improvements which gradually advance and are regularly reviewed, they may be a mechanism to create that sense of urgency. As they are achieved they will undoubtedly help the team to push on as there is nothing like success to improve team morale – remember the Australian Rules description of the authoritarian manager – "good team spirit - when winning".

For a team that has not been successful, the benefit of winning even a secondary competition cannot be underestimated. At a national level one frequently hears comments around the National League finals about how a win is much more important to one of the participants than the other. That is said of the team which has had little success and is an acknowledgement of the fact that a win in this secondary competition will help build confidence in such a team.

Another example is the League Cup in English soccer. This has become something of an irrelevancy to the top teams who frequently field many second team players just to give them game time and experience. But an outright win in this competition is still a big deal for many Premier League clubs who have no real chance of winning the Premier League itself.

I can think of no greater example of this than that described in a Brian Clough biography (*Provided You Don't Kiss Me - 20 years with Brian Clough*, by Duncan Hamilton). In his time at Nottingham Forest, Clough had won promotion to the top division (then the First Division now the Premier League), a couple of League Cups, a First

Division (Premier League today) title and two European Cups (now called Champions Leagues).

These were incredible, unequalled achievements for such a relatively small club, but his most important success, in his own words, was none of these. The first trophy Forest won under his management was a little remembered and hardly mourned competition called the Anglo-Scottish Cup.

It was something many managers would have left off their CV. But its significance to Brian Clough was that it was their first trophy. It gave them the experience of winning. It gave them confidence and it gave him confidence that his methods would work. Consequently, Clough would regard this very minor competition as the most important win of his career – because without it what followed would not have been possible.

When setting short-term goals make sure they are achievable and remember they can be updated regularly as you progress. Make sure they are realistic. Recently, I read an example of a county hurling manager of a (justifiably) unfancied team telling his players they would be hurling in September.

As the All Ireland final is played on the first Sunday in September, this can only be described as an utterly unrealistic goal. The team does not figure in anyone's list of the top six hurling teams of the moment – with the exception of the manager's list. While positivity is to be encouraged, there is no point in setting or agreeing targets which are completely unrealistic.

Note the word of caution in the above description of a business-like manager of whom it is said, "may set goals too high for some team members." If your championship is a group system, you may have "emerging from the group" as a short-term target, later to be revised to reaching a quarter-final or semi-final. If your main competition is a league, consider your targets and whether they should be consolidation, a top six or top four finish or perhaps winning the competition is a reasonable objective.

Equally, a long-term goal is important but it can be more an aspiration. Long-term goals become the eventual outcome if your short-term goals are achieved. Long-term will probably include winning the primary competition for your sport, perhaps a championship, the ultimate ambition of most clubs.

Finally, in their book, *The Mind Gym*, Gary Mack and David Casstevens provide an acronym for goal-setting:

S. Specific
M. Measurable
A. Achievable
R. Realistic
T. Time-bound

SMART: it seems as good a summary as any for setting goals.

SUMMARY

1. Mental preparation is universally acknowledged as having importance

2. Sports psychology can help

3. Goal-setting and achieving consistency are specific areas where benefits can be derived.

4. Dealing with fear and anxiety may be even more beneficial

5. If you do not have regular access to a professional, at least arrange one exploratory meeting/discussion.

CHAPTER 15

SUCCESSION MANAGEMENT PLANNING

"Apres moi, le deluge." After me, the deluge – Louis XV of France or Madame de Pompadour

This is the one subject in these pages, which is not aimed directly at you, the manager or prospective manager. Instead it is included as a topic which, I believe, could be beneficially studied across many sports. The targets for these words are the administrators, professional and amateur, the county chairmen and club chairmen.

A very obvious area where I believe there is a demonstrable need for planning succession is in professional football. The only easily recalled example of a club which actually practised succession management is Liverpool from the days of Bill Shankly to Bob Paisley, Joe Fagan to Kenny Dalglish. All of the replacement managers came from within. And success continued smoothly in the 1970s and 80s.

It is ironic that Liverpool hired Roy Hodgson in 2010, paying Fulham a reported £2m in compensation. He replaced Rafa Benitez who was said to have been paid £4m to go. Within six months of Hodgson's appointment, he was dismissed and was said to have been paid a further £4m in severance compensation. One newspaper report estimated the complete bill for hiring and firing Roy

Hodgson came to around £20m. This included dispensing with and replacing the backroom team. It is hardly a coincidence that Liverpool struggled during this period while they dominated in the days when they were said to have a supply chain of good managers coming through their famous "bootroom".

Meanwhile in the summer of 2011, as another top club, Chelsea, once more changed managers, dismissing Carlo Ancelotti and replacing him with André Villas-Boas, media reports indicate the costs for the changes incurred by the club from the dismissal of Jose Mourinho to this latest appointment, exceed £40m.

When did you last hear of a top professional football team promote someone who was groomed over time for the top management job within the club? Okay, just Barcelona then – and how has that worked out? I do not mean appointing the assistant manager or the head coach to replace a suddenly departed (usually expensively fired) manager. That is not succession management. It is usually simply an expeditious means of filling the vacancy without getting back on the treadmill of recruiting, poaching, then compensating a new appointee as well as the club he is leaving.

Very often the club has to dispense with the backroom team of the departed manager while hiring a new backroom team, selected by the new manager. Actually, when you write it like that, it is even more incredible how expensive a failed managerial appointment can be. And we have not even got to the bit where the new guy wants rid of players brought in by the previous incumbent and wants a big budget to buy his idea of suitable players.

In Gaelic football and hurling the outside manager has become a topical and occasionally a controversial factor. Not many have enjoyed great success. Where have we seen any evidence of good succession planning? There is little evidence that it happens at county level, John Allen succeeding Donal O'Grady in Cork being a rare exception, and it certainly does not occur to any degree at club level.

While we live in a different world to that occupied by the people described in the preceding paragraphs, there is, I believe, a strong case to be made for succession management at both county and club levels. The leadership for such a development will have to come from county boards. The incentive is the removal of the mad scramble to find a manager when the current one fails, retires or simply tires of the task.

I may have already answered the question as to how likely is it that this might happen. After all the basis of this book is my concern that management training is not deemed worthy of consideration, while coaching is the be-all and end-all. How then might we expect boards of counties and clubs to look at providing for their future managerial needs when they pay so little attention to current needs, until a problem arises?

Look at some of the appointments of outside managers to county teams. Ask yourself was there no one within that county capable of doing the job. There may be an argument for bringing a high-profile person in to a weaker county but it is my contention that strong counties recruiting outside managers is an admission of failure. Ask yourself one simple question, in relation to GAA management. "Is it possible that for the past decade there has been no one Waterford hurling person capable of managing the Waterford county hurling team?" That is just the most obvious example of a county which has had a succession of outside managers and of which the question "why?" needs to asked and answered. Contrast that with a club like Nemo Rangers which continues to enjoy success under a succession of home-grown managers.

Until such time as those who govern sporting organisations take seriously the need to select, train and develop potential managers, avoidable problems will continue to cost money and time. Within the GAA, so much is done well. Coaching of players from an early age has long been recognised as a necessity. How effectively this is carried out is a separate matter which needs study and review. A planned approach to the provision of suitably prepared managers at club level would, I believe, bring about significant benefits to county administrations. With an internal supply of qualified managers, the need to look outside would diminish and should disappear entirely. That should be welcome news for many administrations. Bringing about the change is within their capability. A recognition that a problem exists would be a good start as that is usually the first necessary step in coming up with a solution.

Some of what I have written as advice to club managers draws from good practices in business. I am not contending that sport should apply business practices wherever possible. I trust it is clear that I am simply looking at some aspects of business which work well and which might be applied in a sports context.

Businesses do not always cover themselves in glory in dealing with succession management but increasingly, it is becoming an important factor. Analysis in the US shows that organisations with a clear succession plan actually perform better than those who do not have such a plan. In Ireland, the Chambers Ireland website has some interesting observations on this subject: They contend that when (in the business environment) people try to evaluate high-potential performers they frequently don't look beyond some basic characteristics, all of which can be taught in any case. Examples are interpersonal skills and ability to manage others. However, a bit more is required and should be sought, such as: "Multi-tasking in ambiguous situations; consistent temperament and energy level to take the organisation through uncertain times; managing a team to meet specific objectives; maintaining high team morale."

These views come under the heading, "not looking beyond the most obvious criteria when evaluating high-potential performers." However, it appears to me that Chambers Ireland, of all bodies, does a pretty good job in describing several of the necessary traits of a successful manager of a football or hurling team.

Perhaps, when the world of sports takes a more enlightened view on management appointments and management training it might move on some day to completing the exercise and taking a long look at succession management planning. Professional sports outfits could save millions while counties and even clubs could avoid some chaotic, albeit highly entertaining, processes.

A last word from the US where succession management is a hot topic in many business sectors. It is argued that women are much better than men at dealing with the subject. The story goes that Tom was an only son of an extremely wealthy man. He discovered his father was unwell and would live no more than a year or two. Tom decided he should get himself a wife with whom he could share his inheritance when it would arrive. He went off to a social function and met this most beautiful creature whom he proceeded to chat up. Eventually he told her: "I may not look that impressive to you now, but let me tell you my dad is coming to the end of his days and within the next couple of years I will inherit $30m." She listened attentively, took his business card and within a fortnight she became his step-mother!

SUMMARY

1. Any well-run organisation will constantly plan ahead.

2. Sporting bodies or clubs should be no different.

3. Potential managers should be identified early and developed over time.

4. Maybe women are better at succession management.

CHAPTER 16
CAN YOU MANAGE NOW?

Remember management is not about knowing everything. That is not a requirement. Managers in business are not necessarily experts on the different aspects of the business they run. They do require a fundamental knowledge, but the chief executive officer or managing director will not be an expert in finance, accounting, sales, marketing, production, human relations, public relations etc. Typically, the managing director will have come from one of those areas and will have in-depth knowledge of that aspect of the business. For all the other sectors, he/she will depend on the head of the department to run that sector or department efficiently.

It is no different in team management. The manager should have some knowledge of how to deal with each of the tasks that face a management team. As in the commercial world, the manager may not have the answer to a particular question but the competent manager will know where to look for that answer. A good manager will know how to handle problems, how not to panic under pressure.

A competent manager will know when someone in the management team or the playing team needs help. To become that experienced and competent takes time and it takes some training and learning on the job, preferably at a lower level before progressing. Ideally, the manager of the football team has coached and has developed a deep knowledge of the game well ahead of stepping into management. It also takes hard work. But doesn't anything worthwhile?

SEEK ADVICE

I have long lived by the principle that if I do not have the expertise in a specific area, I seek advice. This might seem an obvious view to take but it is amazing how many people in sport as well as in business will show reluctance to admit they need help. Whether it is dietary advice, a weights programme, or some aspect of mental preparation, get the right advice and don't try to "wing" it.

This particular belief is based on hard experience. In the eighties, I was involved in setting up a new business. Things went well and relatively soon after we got the business off the ground we were approached by an overseas company who wished to sell us their Irish manufacturing plant. We entered an exclusivity agreement with them which precluded them from talking to anyone else until our talks reached a conclusion. We were quite interested in doing the deal but progress was slow.

Eventually, while on a business trip, I took a call from my business partner, in my hotel in Italy. He informed me that the other side had broken the exclusivity agreement and were engaged in talks with the plant manager who had got to hear that the factory was for sale. We were outraged that an internationally known, reputable company could behave in this way. Our response was to become indignant and offended by this clear breach of etiquette and good manners. Because that was how we saw it, and because we did not seek outside legal advice, we immediately wrote to our contact pointing out his treachery and withdrawing from the talks.

Had we stopped to think or had we got advice we would of course have seen what had occurred as a breach of contract as opposed to a breach of good manners. As we discovered to our horror, a breach of contract could have been a very costly experience for the other company and, financially, a very beneficial matter for us. It was a mistake.

But life is littered with mistakes and as long as they are not fatal and the lesson is learned, we can move on and learn from the experience so we don't repeat the error. From that experience, I have always sought advice rather than dive in with a response.

TRUST

There is one word which I have saved until the end and which describes something that is critical to your efforts to build the relationship between you as manager and your players. That word is "trust".

If you are open and honest and respectful; if you communicate clearly; if you treat people fairly and demonstrate how you will lead with hard work, you will go a long way towards building the trust which is the bedrock upon which your relationship with your players must be built.

Whatever your sport, I hope you have found something useful in this book. Now that you have thought about managing a club team, I wish you well in your decision and in your time in management. Always remember, nothing worthwhile is easy and only one team can win any competition.

SURVEY

A survey carried out in early 2011, among Gaelic footballers and hurlers, asked the following questions:

1. What are the three most important qualities/characteristics you would like to see in the manager of your club team?

2. What are the three worst traits you have encountered in a manager of your club team?

The top 10 qualities the players would like to see are ranked here in order of importance:

1. Leadership/motivational ability.

2. Man-management skills/approachability.

3. Knowledge of the game/good on tactics.

4. Organisational ability/professional approach.

5. Commitment.

6. Fairness.

7. Honesty.

8. Good communication.

9. Positivity/enthusiasm.

10. Commanding respect.

The 10 worst traits players said they had encountered in a manager of their club team were:

1. Lack of organisation.

2. Arrogance/egotism.

3. Lack of fairness/favouritism.

4. Lack of man-management skills.

5. No plan, system or structure to training sessions.

6. Unassertive/lacking authority.

7. Lack of knowledge of game/no ideas or tactical ability.
8. Lack of honesty.
9. Too much talking and inability to listen.
10. Ignorance/aggression/bad language.

I would contend that the negative points were easier to express as they reflect actual experiences whereas the positive list, the qualities a player would ideally like to find in the club manager, require more thought, before putting into words the ideal qualities of a manager. However with a sample of 300 answers I believe this is a reasonable summary of how the modern-day player feels.

It is interesting to note that players listed leadership and motivational ability as the foremost requirement in a manager of their club team. They wish to be led and motivated and as the 10th point states they actually want a manager who commands respect. These topics have been covered in this book and the survey shows their importance to players.

The second most important ranked requirement is man-management ability/approachability. One of my expressed views on the recent high-profile rows in the GAA is that in some cases a coach, perhaps an excellent coach, was appointed manager without any managerial training or background. The discovery that he had no managerial ability always came too late and at too high a cost and usually manifested itself in a fatal lack of man management skills.

The requirement for a "knowledge of the game and

tactics" is interesting in that it confirms the need for someone entering club management to have acquired this knowledge from experience in coaching and in other areas prior to taking on the job. In an ideal world this is what players want. Organisational ability is the fourth ranked most desirable quality players seek in their manager. Interestingly, on the list of negative experiences, the lack of organisational ability was rated the worst trait encountered by players.

Perhaps, it is a characteristic which is better appreciated by players when they encounter a manager devoid of organisational skills – maybe players don't realise how important this facet of management is until they are subjected to someone devoid of organisational ability. In my own playing days I recall the absolute shambles experienced through having a manager of whom it was said he would have difficulty making certain arrangements in a brewery.

It might be expected that the manager's commitment could be taken for granted but players seem to rate the requirement quite highly in fifth place. It may be that in an age where many clubs appoint outside managers, what motivates such people is being called into question by players.

Fairness appears as the sixth most important requirement but tellingly Lack of Fairness/ Favouritism comes in third place among players' worst experiences. Favouritism appears to be a common complaint among players and I have no doubt there is a high incidence of unfairness on the part of inadequate managers. I would say if the accusation is justified it reflects a serious weakness of character in a manager. It may also be that there is a possibility that some players will perceive favouritism where it might not really exist. Players are not always their own worst critics and most of us have come across the player who could not understand why he was not more highly rated by management. So while favouritism or unfairness is unforgiveable, the charge may not always be valid.

The next most sought after quality is Honesty and that is linked to the same issues as Fairness although Honesty probably covers a wider area. It is of course a valid requirement. This is borne out by the choice of Lack of Honesty in the list of the 10 worst traits encountered, where it is placed at number eight.

Communication has been well covered and is undoubtedly critical if a successful relationship is to be established between manager and players.

The next trait "Positivity/Enthusiasm" can probably be linked to "Commitment" in this context as it is hard to envisage someone being credited with possessing either commitment or enthusiasm, without the other.

Among the other negative traits, the worst experiences listed by players put "arrogance/egotism" in second place behind "lack of organisation". I found this a little surprising but evidently there are more pompous and opinionated people operating in club management than

I had imagined. In any walk of life, sport or work, no one likes to find him/herself reporting to an arrogant, egotistical person.

The other extreme of "Unassertiveness and Lack of Authority" is also high on the list of bad traits encountered. I have no doubt that finding a person of this type has been appointed to manage your team must be extremely disheartening because you know from the start it is not going to work out.

The remaining negative characteristics experienced were the manager who talks too much and cannot listen, and the manager who is ignorant and aggressive with the use of bad language specifically mentioned by several players in relation to the latter. People talking and not listening are all too common prompting the comment about why we get two ears and only one mouth. Ignorance and Aggression are probably linked to the Arrogance which was the second worst trait as voted by the players in this survey.

While the players' requirements and their bad experiences may have been predictable it is interesting to see the order in which they are ranked. The results of the survey simply point out what players think and feel about how they would like to be treated as well as the type of approach which has been unacceptable to them in the past and which should be unacceptable forever if management is to provide the enlightened leadership which is essential for the well-being of the game and those who play it.

In summary, the survey demonstrates that players wish to be led and inspired, treated fairly and in a civil manner. They expect the manager to manage, to be well organised, to ensure training sessions are well run and enjoyable and to be provided with some tactical guidance that makes sense because clearly it is the product of some applied intelligence. It does not seem a lot to ask for. It contains nothing unreasonable and a number of things which should be provided without question or hesitation if the game and those who play it are to be respected for their efforts and properly led, motivated and managed. Which leads us back to the question, can you fulfil these needs? Can you manage?

BIBLIOGRAPHY

Books to which reference has been made.

"Moneyball: The Art of Winning an Unfair Game" Michael Lewis (2003 W W Norton & Co)

"Lion Man" Ian McGeechan (2009 Simon & Schuster)

"The Art of Captaincy" (1985 Hodder & Stoughton Ltd)

"Wooden on Leadership" John Wooden and Steve Jamison (2005 McGraw Hill)

"The Economics of Football" Stephen Dobson and John Goddard (2001 Cambridge University Press)

"Screaming at the Sky - My Journey" Tony Griffin with T.J.Flynn (2010 Transworld Ireland)

"Inverting the Pyramid – A History of Football Tactics" Jonathan Wilson (2008 Orion Books)

"The Club" Christy O'Connor (2010 Penguin Ireland)

"Keys to the Kingdom" Jack O'Connor (2007 Penguin Books)

"The Will to Win" Seán Boylan–The Autobiography as told to John Quinn (2006 The O'Brien Press Ltd.)

"Presence Is The Only Thing" Mickey Harte with Michael Foley (2009 Poolbeg Books Ltd)

"Rebound Rules" Rick Pitino with Pat Forde (2008 HarperCollins)

"Rebel Rebel" The Billy Morgan Story with Billy Keane (2009 Ballpoint Press)

"Mind Gym" Gary Mack with David Casstevens (2001 McGraw Hill)

"Pure Sport" Practical Sport Psychology John Kremer and Aidan P.Moran (2008 Routledge)

"Provided You Don't Kiss Me - 20 Years With Brian Clough" Duncan Hamilton (2007 Fourth Estate)

"Outliers" Malcolm Gladwell (2008 Little, Brown and Company)

APPENDIX

ACKNOWLEDGEMENTS AND THANKS

I have learned the hard way that there are different phases to writing and publishing a book. I offer my heartfelt thanks to those who encouraged me from the very beginning of this exercise: Clare Healy, Barbara, Clare C and Patrick Healy, Aodhagan Hurley, Peter Morrissey and Fiona Whelan.

I would especially like to acknowledge the following groups of people for their inestimable help in writing and producing the book you hold in your hand...

To those who offered valuable help and practical guidance and assistance in making this a viable project: Pat Daly, Noel Murphy, Dave Billings, Paul Towell and Jimmy Dunne, whose wide knowledge and support covered several aspects of this exercise.

To the sports people who helped in various ways with research: John McClean, Peter Keegan, Colette Forde, Declan Griffin, Mick Shelley and Matt Britton.

To the people directly involved with publishing this book: Joe Coyle for his Trojan design work as well as his great patience, and the ever-encouraging PJ Cunningham, whose editorial advice and input were invaluable.

To Billy Morgan and Pat Devlin for their positive and helpful comments and especially Eugene McGee for taking the time to read the original manuscript and for his very helpful advice.

Finally to those people with whom I walked the line with

various teams over the years, thanks for the great memories and for the enduring friendships...

At Bray Emmets: Brendan Devitt, Declan O'Neill, Michael Broderick, Ian Gourley, Gerry Walsh, Ger Lenihan, Ronan Matthews, Des Kelly, Mick Ryan and the world's greatest clubman, Tom Walsh.

At Castletown: Tommy Masterson, Glen O'Kelly and the inestimable Joe Sullivan.

At Wicklow: Mick O'Toole, Jim McCormack and Brian McBride. Joe Sullivan and Glen O'Kelly were also part of that management team.

At UCD: Gerry McGill, Eamon Prenter, Malachy O'Rourke, Stephen Gallagher, the irrepressible Billy Sheehan and the only man I know whose speed-dial listing is actually bigger than the phonebook, the boss, Dave Billings.